Winning Softball Drills

A Complete Drill Book for Coaches

Dianne I. Baker
Dr. Sandra S. Cole

**Championship Books
and Video Productions**
2730 Graham
Ames, Iowa 50010
1-800-873-2730

Library of Congress Catalog Card Number: 91-072843

ISBN: 1-880138-00-X

Cover Design: Andre Kriel

Photography: Hardy Meredith

Published by:

Championship Books
and Video Productions
2730 Graham
Ames, Iowa 50010
1-800-873-2730

Preface

Winning Softball Drills: A Complete Drill Book for Coaches was born from a need expressed by both high school and collegiate softball coaches for a working manual to help them produce drills quickly for all aspects of the game. The result was the development of over 200 drills and ideas, explained in detail and illustrated with easy-to-understand diagrams, offering information ranging from basic fundamentals to total team concepts. The goals of this book are twofold. First, it is intended to help coaches get the most from their athletes during practices through the use of specific drills, and secondly, to help coaches produce organized and time-efficient practices. It is not our intention to pass on a particular coaching philosophy. You can select specific drills to fit your team's needs and adapt those drills accordingly.

Careful consideration was given to the book's design. The book is intended to be rugged enough to be carried to practice every day, and handy enough for you to have diagrams and drills at your fingertips. The subjects in the photographs represent male and female coaches. We felt it was important for coaches to demonstrate the drills since they are the ones who teach the athletes the fundamentals of the game.

The drills have been designed to be time efficient and to enhance learning by correct repetition. We are committed to the idea that fundamental skills are essential to winning. The more the players practice the drills correctly, the more they will learn, and the better prepared they will be to react in game situations. It is our hope that by using **Winning Softball Drills: A Complete Drill Book for Coaches**, your players and your program will have that winning edge that comes from excellence in fundamentals and strategy concepts.

Dianne I. Baker

Sandra S. Cole

Dianne I. Baker is Assistant Athletic Director at Stephen F. Austin State University and has finished her 11th year as Head Softball Coach. Under her guidance the Ladyjacks have captured one NCAA national title, two NCAA regional titles, two Gulf Star Conference titles, and one Southland Conference title. Her career record is 414-178. Coach Baker has been honored on numerous occasions including being named NSCA National and Regional Coach of the year in 1986 and the Gulf Star Conference Coach of the year in 1984. She received her Bachelor of Science Degree from Texas Woman's University and her Master of Education Degree from Stephen F. Austin State University. Coach Baker is a noted clinician and has written numerous articles on softball conditioning programs and practice organization.

Dr. Sandra S. Cole is a Professor of Kinesiology and Health Science at Stephen F. Austin State University. She earned her Doctor of Physical Education Degree from Indiana University with specialization in biomechanics. She has an extensive background in studying and analyzing the mechanics of sports. Dr. Cole has served as a consultant in developing softball circuit training and weight training conditioning programs and in formulating softball drill designs.

Contents

4 Outfielders' Drills 79

5 Pitching Programs and Drills 103

Legend

The following symbols are applicable to the drills illustrated throughout the text of this book.

(HC) – Head Coach

(AC) – Assistant Coach

(M) – Manager

(1B) – First Baseman

(2B) – Second Baseman

(3B) – Third Baseman

(SS) – Shortstop

(LF) – Left Fielder

(CF) – Center Fielder

(RF) – Right Fielder

(P) – Pitcher

(C) – Catcher

(IF) – Infielder

(OF) – Outfielder

(H) – Hitter

(R) – Runner

(S) – Shagger

(T) – Tosser

◯ – Player

◌ Player's New Position

⟶ Movement of Player

– – – → Path of Thrown Ball

•••••◇ Path of Hit Ball

● Ball

◼ Base

⅄ Pitching Machine

⊔ Ball Bucket

⊤ Batting Tee

▨ Protective Screen

1

Practice Organization

Do you ever wonder why some coaches seem to be successful year after year, and others aren't? One of the main factors that contributes to the success of these coaches is they have the ability to properly organize their practice sessions to meet both daily and long-range goals. Successful coaches realize there are no shortcuts to success. Games are won by hours of hard work in well-planned, organized practices. These coaches accept the fact that their teams will "play like they practice". Their coaching philosophy is simple. They believe if their team is the best trained, best disciplined, and most skillful, their team will win.

Getting Started

Before you start writing practice schedules, you must first identify your own coaching philosophy. Your philosophy will have a lot to do with the drills you select and the time you spend on particular drills. Second, determine how much time you have for practice prior to the first game. This will give you a time range from which to work. Third, evaluate the skill level and knowledge of your players before making the drill selections. It is important for the players to have success in practice. Fourth, prepare a technical skills checklist, which lists all the skills to be covered during the season. By using a checklist system, you are able to keep track of all the material introduced and avoid neglecting some important skills that should be practiced. A sample technical skills checklist can be found on the following page. Adjustments may need to be made to the technical skills checklist depending upon your team's needs.

Technical Skills Checklist

Material to be Covered	Introduction Date	Review Dates

1. Basic fundamentals
2. Fundamentals in playing positions
3. Covering bases/tags
4. Double plays
5. Infield/outfield fly ball jurisdiction
6. Cut-offs/relays
7. Pitching technique
8. Catching technique
9. Hitting technique
10. Bunts (offense)
11. Baserunning
12. Sliding
13. Bunts (defense)
14. Hit and run
15. Bunt and run
16. 1st and 3rd double steals (offense and defense)
17. Pick-offs
18. Rundowns
19. Pre-game warm-up
20. Conditioning
21. Signals

After completing a technical skills checklist, you are ready to prepare a practice schedule. It is a good policy to write the practices down, so you will plan your practices to meet both daily and long-range goals. Your daily practice schedule should consist of all the fundamentals and team strategy drills you wish to cover in a particular day. The daily practice schedule also allows you to keep track of the time spent on each drill, and, therefore, minimizes wasted time. Careful consideration should be given to your selection of drills. Drills are designed for a specific purpose. Decide what is needed by your team and select your drills accordingly. The following is a sample practice schedule which may need to be adjusted depending upon your particular coaching situation.

Practice Schedule

Date:_____ September 1

Late Today:_____ None

Absent Today:_____ All Present

Announcements:_____ Practice Tomorrow 4:15

Equipment Duty:_____ Group 1

Pre-Practice:_____ Pitching Program

Time	Drill	Objective	Group
2:30-2:55	Stretching Program	Warm-up	Everyone
2:55-3:00	Jogging	Warm-up	Everyone
3:00-3:30	Running Drills	Speed/movement	Everyone
	A. Stride-high knee alternate Speed x 4 full outfield	Warm-up	Everyone
	B. Indian Relay	Sprint Work	Two Groups of 8
	C. Explosive Power Drill	Explosive Power	Everyone
3:30-3:50	Hitting Technique	Hitting Technique	Everyone
3:50-4:05	Hitting Drills	Hitting Technique	Infield Only
	1. Stride 4. Resistance Swing	and Strength	
	2. Lead Arm 5. Wrist Snap		
	3. Back Arm 6. Wrist Roller		
4:05-4:20	Throwing Drills	Throwing Technique	Everyone
	A. Easy Throws		
	B. One-Knee		
	C. Easy Throws (30-40-50)		
4:20-4:50	Strength Drills	Conditioning	Outfield Only
	A. Sit-ups D. Jump-ups		
	B. Push-ups E. Pick-ups		
	C. Hops F. Movement Drills		
4:50-5:15	Interval Training	Conditioning	Everyone
	3 x 40 3 x 80 Walk between each rep		
	3 x 60 3 x 60 2 mins between each set		
	3 x 80 3 x 40		
	3 x 110		

Other factors to consider so your practice sessions run smoothly and efficiently are as follows:

1. Prior to the first practice session of the week, prepare the entire week's daily practice schedules. Evaluate your progress after each practice session and make changes accordingly.
2. Organize the practice sessions so each player is accounted for during every minute of the workout.
3. Establish a practice routine with which the athlete can become familiar.
4. Start the practice sessions with fundamental drills and end them with team strategy drills.
5. Introduce new material early in the practice sessions.
6. Emphasize the objective of each drill and explain in detail how to perform the drill.
7. Vary the drills used during the day and from day to day to prevent boredom.
8. Provide enough equipment to keep the drills moving at a steady pace.
   a. Purchase enough ball buckets for each infield position.
   b. Make or purchase several batting tees.
   c. Purchase a batting cage and a pitching machine if your program has the funds.
   d. Make or purchase protective screens for the pitchers and fielders.
9. Have a pitching area for each pitcher on the team.
10. Do not continue the same drill for too long.
11. Have a good manager.
12. Give your manager a copy of the practice schedule so needed equipment can be set up prior to practice.
13. Post a copy of the day's practice schedule so your players can know the schedule for the day.
14. Have the practice field in the best possible shape for every practice. This should include watering and dragging the infield.
15. The coach should arrive at the field early to make certain everything is ready for practice.
16. Provide individual and team stretching time prior to the practice sessions.
17. Start your practices on time and try to avoid running overtime.
18. Keep the practice time to a maximum of 2½ - 3 hours, which includes the warm-up time.
19. Close each practice session on a positive note.

FROM THE INFORMATION PRESENTED IN THIS CHAPTER, YOU SHOULD NOW BE BETTER PREPARED TO ORGANIZE TIME-EFFICIENT PRACTICE SESSIONS TO MEET BOTH DAILY AND LONG-RANGE GOALS.

Basic Fundamental Drills

Drills for improving the following basic fundamentals are presented in this chapter:
1. Throwing
2. Fielding ground balls
3. Lateral movement
4. Charging
5. Catching fly balls moving up
6. Catching fly balls over the shoulder
7. Player communication

One-Knee Throwing Drill

Objective:

To develop the player's arm and shoulder strength for throwing.

Set-Up:

Each pair of players kneels on the ground 10 yards apart facing each other. (Right-handed players kneel on the right knee with the left leg out in front, while left-handed players kneel on the left knee with the right leg out in front).

Each pair of players has one ball.

Directions:

The players throw the ball back and forth to each other for a desired time period. Then the players are moved apart another 5 yards, and they continue to throw back and forth to each other for an additional time period. The drill continues to proceed in this manner for as long as desired.

Coaching Hint:

The distance the players are moved apart depends on their arm and shoulder strength.

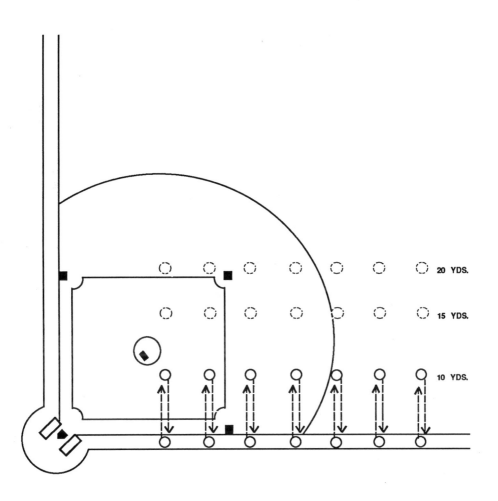

20 YDS.

15 YDS.

10 YDS.

One-Knee Throwing Drill

5 x 5 Basic Fielding Drill

Objective:

To learn the basic fundamentals of fielding.

Set-Up:

Drill has one tosser and one player, who are 12 feet apart facing each other.

Drill can have as many groups as desired.

Directions:

The tosser throws five ground balls to the player, who fields each ball and throws it back to the tosser. The player then moves 12 more feet away from the tosser. This drill sequence continues until the player has fielded five ground balls at five different locations.

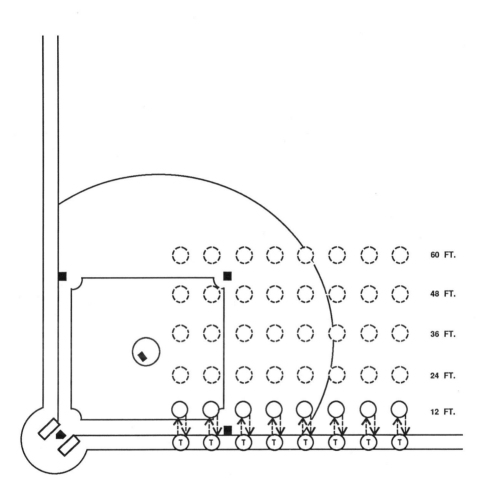

5 x 5 Basic Fielding Drill

Fungo Fielding Drill

Objective:

To provide the players with an opportunity to field a large number of ground balls.

Set-Up:

Drill has one player, who is 60 feet in front of a hitter, and one shagger, who stands on the right side of the hitter.

Drill can have as many groups as desired.

Directions:

The hitter hits 10 ground balls to the player. After fielding the 10 ground balls, the player becomes the shagger, the shagger becomes the hitter, and the hitter becomes the new player. The drill continues to proceed in this manner for as long as desired.

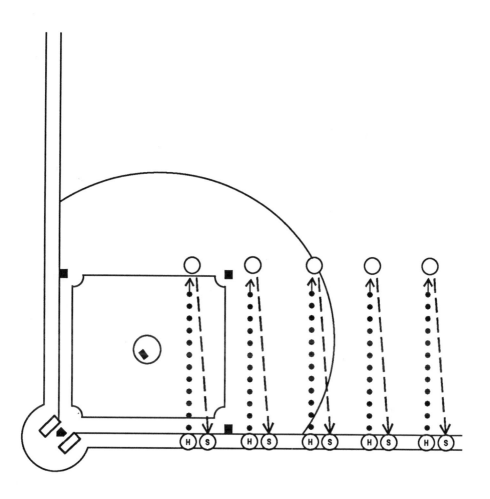

Fungo Fielding Drill

Lateral Movement Drill #1

Objective:

To improve the player's ability to move laterally and to assume a good defensive position in fielding a ground ball.

Set-Up:

Drill has six balls placed between first base and second base and six balls placed between second base and third base.

Drill can be performed by three to five players at a time for each six-ball arrangement.

Directions:

One group starts in a defensive position between first base and second base and in front and between balls 3 and 4. The other group starts in a defensive position between second base and third base and in front and between balls 3 and 4. Each group uses a cross-over step to the first ball on the right and jogs back to the starting position, pauses, then uses a cross-over step to the first ball on the left and jogs back to the starting position, pauses, and continues in this manner until all balls have been covered.

Coaching Hint:

It is important that your players maintain a low position while moving to the ball and assume a good defensive position when getting to the ball.

Variation:

The drill is performed with eight balls placed between the bases. The players then assume their defensive positions between balls 4 and 5.

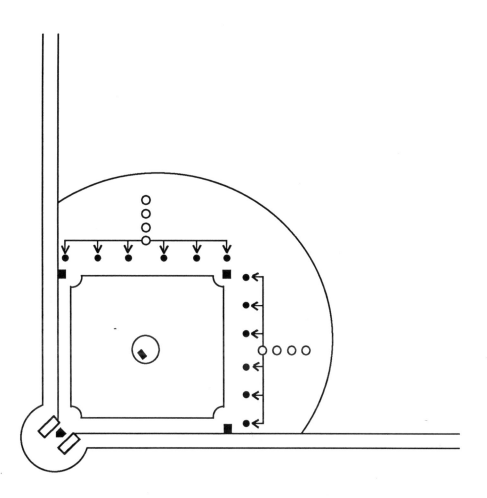

Lateral Movement Drill #1

Lateral Movement Drill #2

Objective:

To improve the player's ability to react and move laterally in fielding a ground ball.

Set-Up:

Drill has two tossers who are near the pitching area.

Each tosser has two shaggers with one standing on each side of the tosser.

Drill can have four or more players in each line.

One line of players is at the second baseman's defensive position, while the other line of players is at the shortstop's defensive position.

Directions:

The tosser throws a ground ball randomly to the right or left of the player making the player move laterally to field the ball. After fielding the ball, the player throws the ball back to the shagger on that side. Then the player turns to the outside and jogs back to the end of the line.

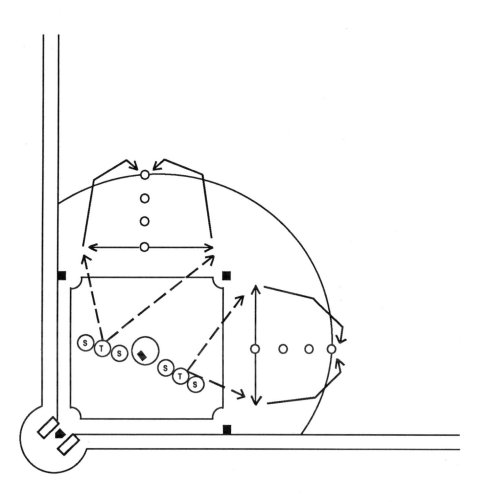

Lateral Movement Drill #2

Lateral Line Drill

Objective:

To improve the player's ability to move into position, field the ball, and make a good throw.

Set-Up:

Drill can have six to eight tossers.
Tossers are spaced 8-10 feet apart with each tosser having a ball.
Drill has one player, who is 50-60 feet in front of tosser 1.

Directions:

Tosser 1 throws a ground ball to the player. The player fields the ball and throws the ball back to tosser 1. As the player moves across and in front of tosser 2, tosser 2 throws a ground ball to the player and times the ball to reach the player as the player reaches the new position. The player fields the ball and throws the ball back to tosser 2. The drill continues until the last tosser throws a ground ball to the player. If the drill for that player is to stop, the player throws the ball back to the last tosser. Then each tosser moves to the left one position, tosser 1 now becomes the player, and the previous player becomes the last tosser in line. If the drill is to continue for the player after receiving a ground ball from the last tosser, the player reverses direction in front of the tossers, and the drill sequence continues until the player gets in front of tosser 1. After fielding the ball, the player throws the ball back to tosser 1, and then becomes the last tosser in line. Tosser 1 now becomes the new player.

Variation:

The tossers throw line drives or fly balls to the player.

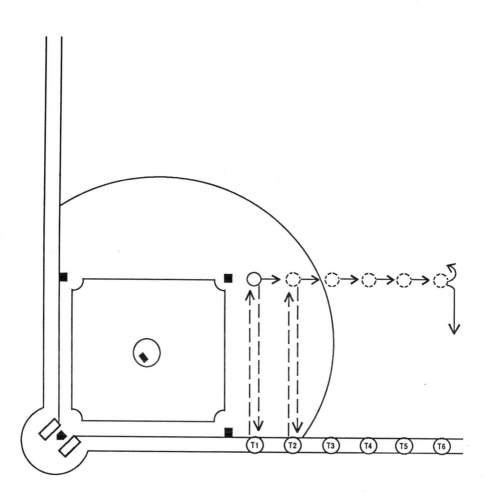

Lateral Line Drill

Lateral Pick-Up Drill

Objectives:

1. To improve the player's overall conditioning.
2. To improve the player's ability to move laterally and to assume a good defensive position in fielding a ground ball.

Set-Up:

Drill has one tosser and one player, who are 6-7 feet apart facing each other.

Drill can have as many groups as desired.

Directions:

The tosser rolls a ball about 5-6 feet out to the side. The player moves on a semicircular path to field the ball. After picking-up the ball, the player throws the ball back to the tosser. The tosser then rolls a ball about 5-6 feet out to the opposite side, and the player fields the ball in a similar manner. The drill sequence is repeated from five to ten times depending on the player's conditioning level. The number of repetitions is increased as the player's conditioning level improves.

Coaching Hint:

It is important for the player to field the ball by moving on a semicircular path in order for the drill to be effective.

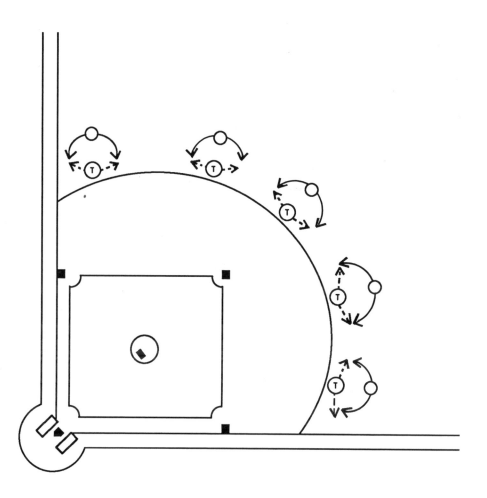

Lateral Pick-Up Drill

Charging Drill

Objective:

To improve the player's ability to charge a softly hit ground ball.

Set-Up:

Drill can have as many tossers as desired.
Drill can have three or more players in the lines, which are about 70 feet in front of the tossers.

Directions:

The tosser throws a ground ball so that the player has to charge the ball at about midway between the tosser and the player. The player then throws the ball back to the tosser, turns to the right, and jogs back to the end of the line.

Variation:

While infielders start about 70 feet in front of the tossers, outfielders should start about 90 feet in front of the tossers. The tosser still attempts to throw the ground ball so that the player has to charge the ball at about midway between the tosser and the player.

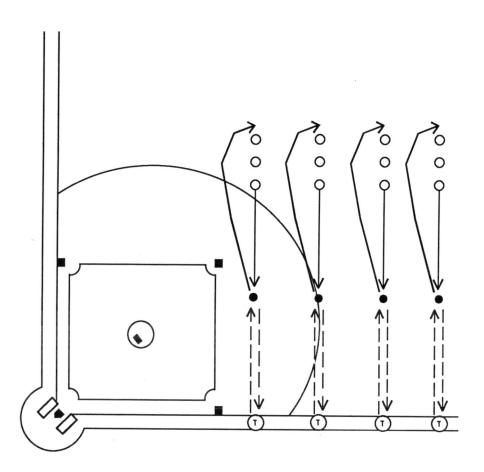

Charging Drill

Fly Ball Drill #1

Objective:

To improve the player's ability to catch a fly ball while moving up.

Set-Up:

Drill has one tosser and one player.
Drill can have as many groups as desired.

Directions:

The player starts 90 feet away from the tosser. The tosser throws a fly ball to around 75 feet where the player must run up to catch or retrieve the ball. The player then throws the ball back to the tosser and runs back to the starting position. The drill continues in the same manner with the tosser throwing the ball to about 60 feet, then 45 feet, then 30 feet, and finally 15 feet. Each time after catching or retrieving the ball, the player throws the ball back to the tosser and then runs back to the starting position.

Coaching Hints:

This is a good drill for early season conditioning in order to increase the player's overall endurance.

Also, this drill can be performed indoors during inclement weather.

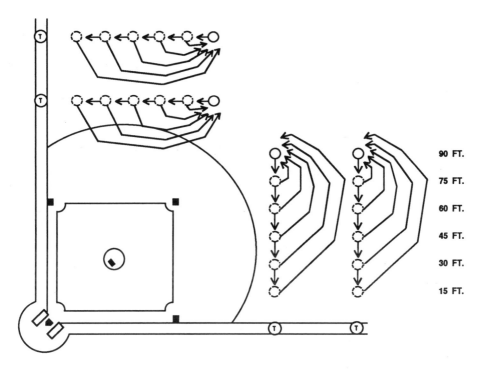

90 FT.

75 FT.

60 FT.

45 FT.

30 FT.

15 FT.

Fly Ball Drill #1

Fly Ball Drill #2

Objective:

To improve the player's ability to catch a fly ball over the shoulder.

Set-Up:

Drill has one tosser and one player.
Drill can have as many groups as desired.

Directions:

The player starts on the side line. The tosser stands on the left side of the player. The player runs out about 15 feet and the tosser leads with a fly ball so that the player has to reach to catch the ball over the left shoulder. After catching or retrieving the ball, the player throws the ball back to the tosser and runs back to the starting position at the line. The drill continues in the same manner with the tosser leading the player out to a spot about 30 feet from the line, then 45 feet, then 60 feet, and finally 75 feet. Each time after catching or retrieving the ball, the player throws the ball back to the tosser and then runs back to the starting position at the line.

Coaching Hints:

This is a good drill for early season conditioning in order to increase the player's overall endurance.

Also, this drill can be performed indoors during inclement weather.

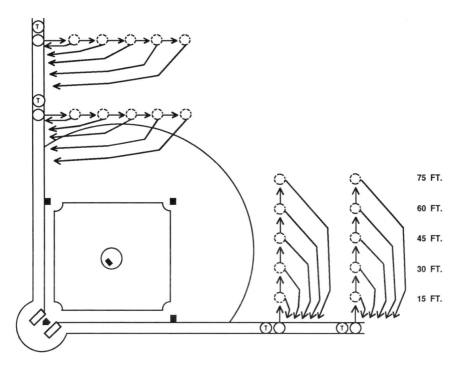

75 FT.

60 FT.

45 FT.

30 FT.

15 FT.

Fly Ball Drill #2

Over-the-Shoulder Catch Drill
(Variation of Fly Ball Drill #2)

Objective:

To improve the player's ability to catch a fly ball over the shoulder.

Set-Up:

Drill can have as many tossers as desired.
Drill can have four or more players in each line.
Each player has a ball.

Directions:

The tosser stands on the left side of the player. The player hands the ball to the tosser, then runs out, and the tosser leads with a fly ball so that the player has to reach to catch the ball over the left shoulder. After catching or retrieving the ball, the player turns to the left, and jogs back to the end of the line.

Variation:

The tosser stands on the right side of the player and throws the ball over the player's right shoulder.

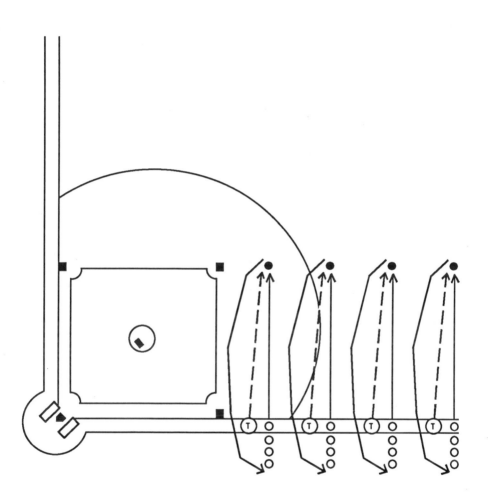

Over-the-Shoulder Catch Drill

Relay Drill

Objectives:

1. To improve the player's ability to field or catch a ball.
2. To improve the player's ability to relay a ball to a specific target.

Set-Up:

Three people are spaced 50 feet apart from each other.
Drill can have as many groups as desired.

Directions:

Tosser 1 throws a ground ball to the player, the player fields the ball, and turns to throw to tosser 2. Tosser 2 throws a ground ball to the player, the player fields the ball, and turns to throw to tosser 1. (Each tosser raises the glove in a manner to present a target for the player.) After the player has received 10 ground balls, the player rotates with one of the tossers, and the drill continues until each person has served as the player.

Variations:

1. The tosser throws line drives randomly to the right or left of the player and the drill proceeds as previously stated.
2. The tosser throws fly balls to the player and the drill proceeds as previously stated.

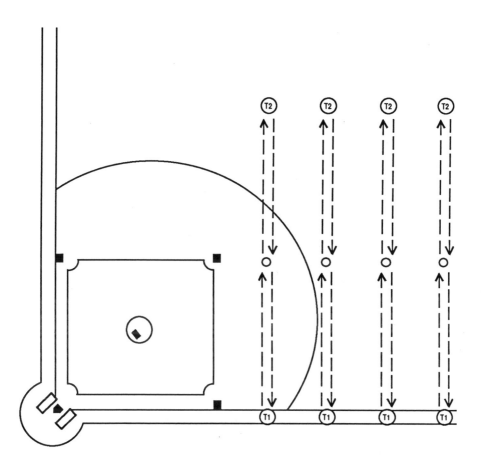

Relay Drill

Double Relay Drill

Objectives:

1. To improve the player's ability to rundown a ball.
2. To improve the player's ability to relay a ball to a specific target.

Set-Up:

Three people are spaced 50 feet apart from each other.
Drill can have as many groups as desired.

Directions:

Tosser 1 starts facing away from the player. Tosser 1 rolls the ball out in front, runsdown the ball, and then turns to throw the ball to the player who acts as the relay person. After catching the ball, the player turns and throws the ball to tosser 2. Tosser 2 then turns away from the player and proceeds in the same manner as tosser 1. (Each tosser raises the glove in a manner to present a target for the player.) After the player has received five throws, the player rotates with one of the tossers, and the drill continues until each person has served as the player.

Coaching Hint:

When the tosser runsdown the ball, have the relay person to turn to the side with the glove hand held high to receive the ball. This procedure allows the relay person to just step and throw, which shortens the relay time.

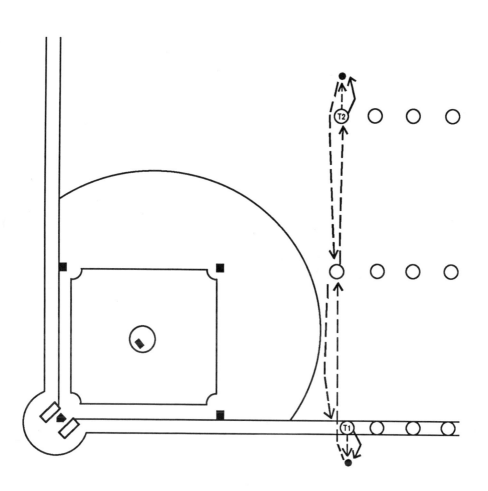

Double Relay Drill

Player Communication Drill #1

Objective:

To improve communication among players when attempting to field or catch the same ball.

Set-Up:

Drill has one tosser who is in front of the pitching area, and one shagger who stands on the right side of the tosser.

Drill can have four or more players in each line.

One line of players is located at the second baseman's defensive position, while the other line of players is at the shortstop's defensive position.

Directions:

The tosser throws a ground ball toward second base and the first players in each line work together in trying to cut-off the ball before it goes into the outfield. The players then jog to the ends of the opposite lines from which they started.

Variation:

The tosser throws a fly ball to the players and the drill proceeds as previously stated.

Coaching Hint for Variation:

At the beginning of the season, it is important for you to establish a fly ball jurisdiction rule. For example, the second baseman would have jurisdiction over the first baseman, and the shortstop would have jurisdiction over the third baseman, etc.

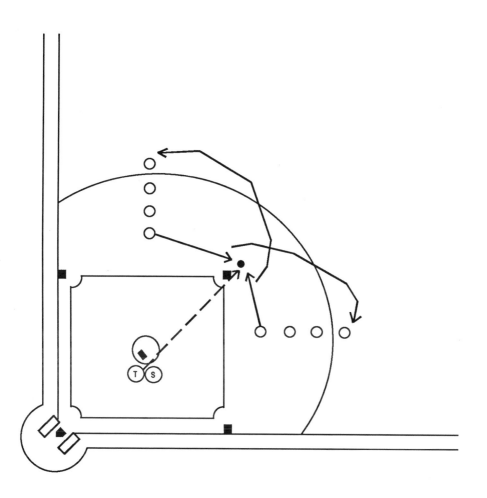

Player Communication Drill #1

Player Communication Drill #2

Objective:

To improve the player's communication with other players when catching balls hit between first-and-second and shortstop-and-third.

Set-Up:

Drill has two tossers who are in front of home plate, and each tosser has a shagger who stands to the right side of the tosser.

Drill can have four or more players in a line.

The lines are located at the defensive positions for the first baseman, second baseman, third baseman, and shortstop.

Directions:

One tosser throws a fly ball in the gap behind first base, while the other tosser throws a fly ball in the gap behind third base. The first players in each group work together when catching the ball. The player who catches the ball throws it back to the shagger, and the players jog back to the ends of their respective lines.

Coaching Hint:

At the beginning of the season, it is important for you to establish a fly ball jurisdiction rule. For example, the second baseman would have jurisdiction over the first baseman, and the shortstop would have jurisdiction over the third baseman, etc.

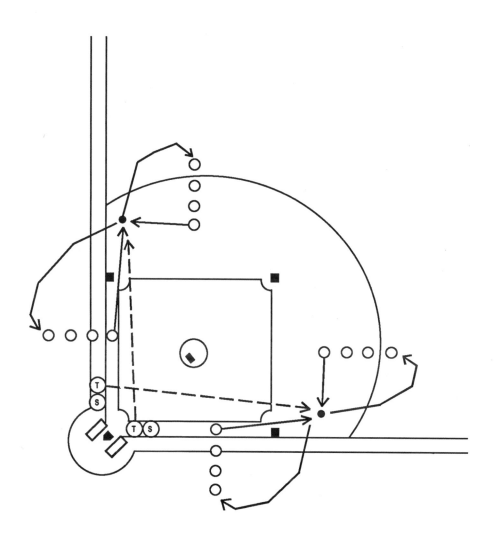

Player Communication Drill #2

From using the drills contained in this chapter, your athletes should improve on the following:

1. Strengthening the arms and shoulders for throwing
2. Fielding fundamentals
3. Moving laterally in fielding a ground ball
4. Charging a softly hit ground ball
5. Catching a fly ball that is hit in front or behind them
6. Communicating with another player when attempting to field or catch the same ball

3

Infielders' Drills

Drills for improving the following infielders' skills are presented in this chapter:
1. Throwing fundamentals
2. Performing fundamentals in playing positions
3. Turning double plays
4. Covering of bases and tags
5. Preventing steal attempts

Star Throwing Drill #1

Objective:

To improve the infielders' throwing accuracy.

Set-Up:

The first baseman and third baseman are at their respective bases, while the catcher, second baseman, and shortstop are at their defensive positions.

Directions:

The ball should be thrown continuously in the following sequence: catcher to second baseman, second baseman to third baseman, third baseman to first baseman, first baseman to shortstop, and shortstop to catcher.

Repeat the drill as many times as desired.

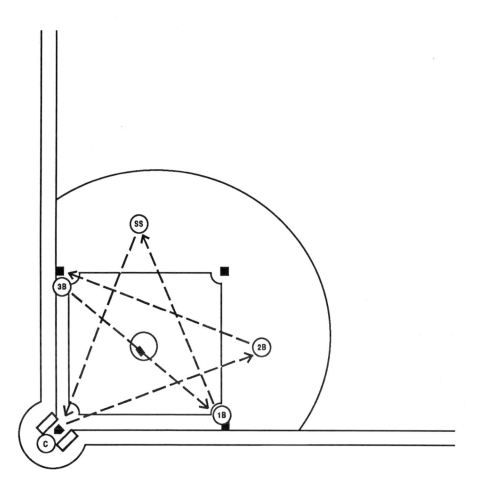

Star Throwing Drill #1

Star Throwing Drill #2

Objective:

To improve the infielders' throwing accuracy.

Set-Up:

The first baseman and third baseman are at their respective bases, while the catcher, second baseman, and shortstop are at their defensive positions.

Directions:

The ball should be thrown continuously in the following sequence: catcher to shortstop, shortstop to first baseman, first baseman to third baseman, third baseman to second baseman, and second baseman to catcher.

Repeat the drill as many times as desired.

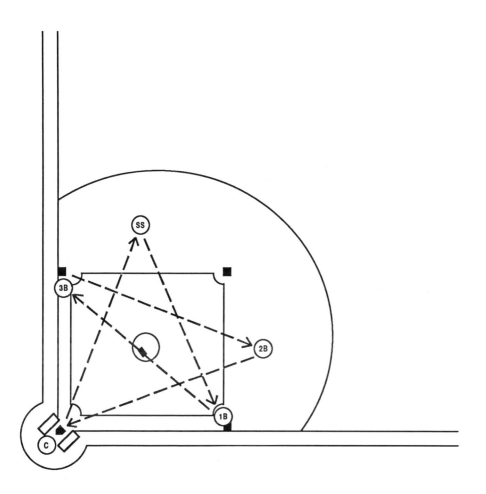

Star Throwing Drill #2

Around the Horn and Reverse
Throwing Drill

Objective:

To improve the infielders' throwing accuracy.

Set-Up:

The catcher, first baseman, and third baseman are at their respective bases.

The second baseman and shortstop are both at second base.

Directions:

The ball should be thrown continuously in the following sequence: catcher to first baseman, first baseman to second baseman, (the shortstop alternates taking throws at second base), second baseman to third baseman, and third baseman to catcher. When the ball reaches the catcher, the drill sequence is reversed around the horn.

Repeat the drill as many times as desired.

Variation:

Each infielder practices making a tag upon receiving the ball.

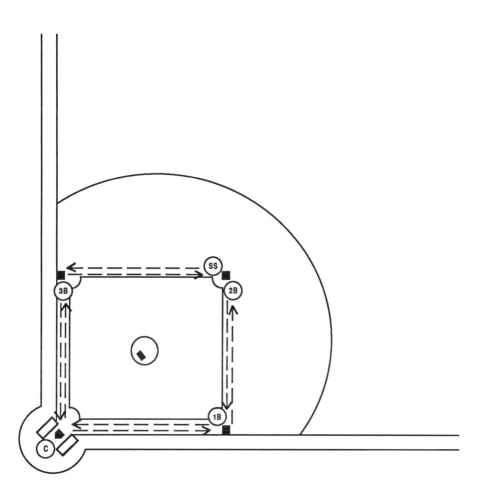

**Around the Horn and Reverse
Throwing Drill**

V Throwing Drill

Objective:

To improve the infielders' throwing accuracy.

Set-Up:

The catcher, first baseman, and third baseman are at their respective bases, while the second baseman and shortstop are at their defensive positions.

Directions:

The ball should be thrown continuously in the following sequence: catcher to first baseman, first baseman to third baseman, third baseman to second base with the second baseman covering the base, second baseman to catcher, catcher to second base with the shortstop covering the base, shortstop to third baseman, and third baseman to catcher.

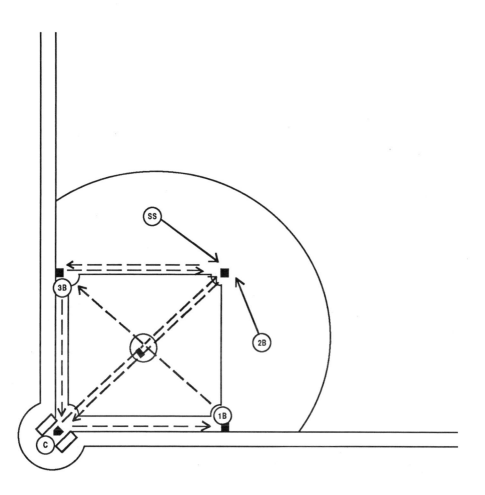

V Throwing Drill

Box Throwing Drill

Objective:

To allow all infielders to practice covering their bases and receiving the ball for tags and forced outs.

Set-Up:

The first baseman and the third baseman are at their respective bases, while the catcher, second baseman, and shortstop are at their defensive positions.

Directions:

The catcher throws the ball to first base, the first baseman throws to third base, the third baseman throws to second base with the second baseman covering the base, and the second baseman throws the ball to the catcher. The catcher throws the ball back to second base with the shortstop covering the base, the shortstop throws the ball to first base, the first baseman throws to third base, and the third baseman throws it back to the catcher.

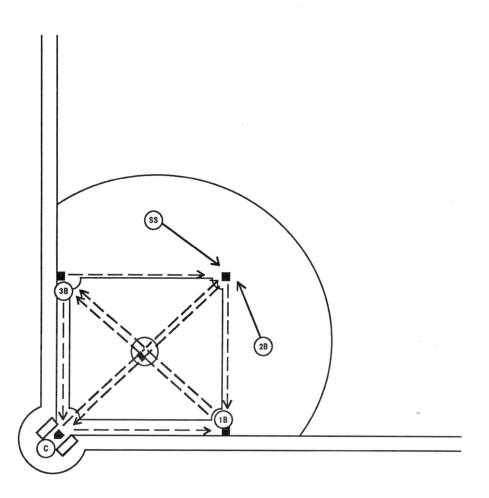

Box Throwing Drill

First Baseman and Shortstop
Fielding Drill

Objective:

To provide the first baseman and shortstop with an opportunity to field a large number of ground balls at their positions and to practice throwing accurately to specific bases.

Set-Up:

Drill has two hitters with one on the right side of home plate and the other on the left side of home plate. Both hitters have a shagger. Each shagger stands on the right side of the hitter and has a bucket of balls.

Empty ball buckets are at first and third bases.

The first baseman, second baseman, third baseman, and the shortstop are at their defensive positions.

Directions:

Hitter 1 hits a ground ball to the shortstop, who fields the ball and throws it to third base.

Hitter 2 hits a ground ball to the first baseman, who fields the ball and throws it to first base with the second baseman covering the base. Since the drill is designed to provide a large number of ground balls to the shortstop and first baseman, allow the second baseman and third baseman to stay at the bases they are covering for the continuation of the drill. The second baseman and third baseman then toss the balls into the empty ball buckets.

The manager should maintain a supply of balls to the shaggers.

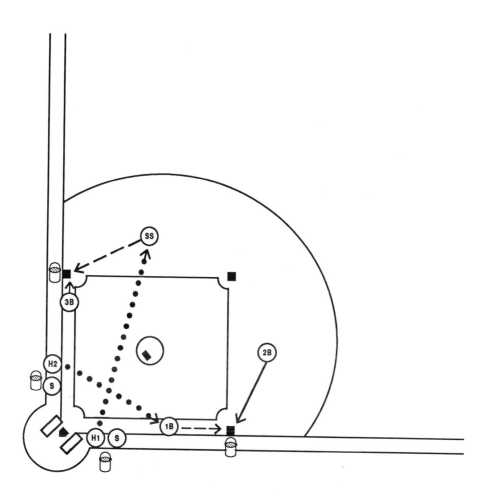

First Baseman and Shortstop
Fielding Drill

Second Baseman and Shortstop Fielding Drill

Objective:

To provide the second baseman and shortstop with an opportunity to field a large number of ground balls at their positions and to practice throwing accurately to specific bases.

Set-Up:

Drill has two hitters with one on the right side of home plate and the other on the left side of home plate. Both hitters have a shagger. Each shagger stands on the right side of the hitter and has a bucket of balls.

Empty ball buckets are at first and third bases.

The first baseman and third baseman are at their respective bases, while the second baseman and shortstop are at their defensive positions.

Directions:

Hitter 1 hits a ground ball to the shortstop, who fields the ball and throws it to third base.

Hitter 2 hits a ground ball to the second baseman, who fields the ball and throws it to first base. The first baseman and third baseman then toss the balls into the empty ball buckets.

The manager should maintain a supply of balls to the shaggers.

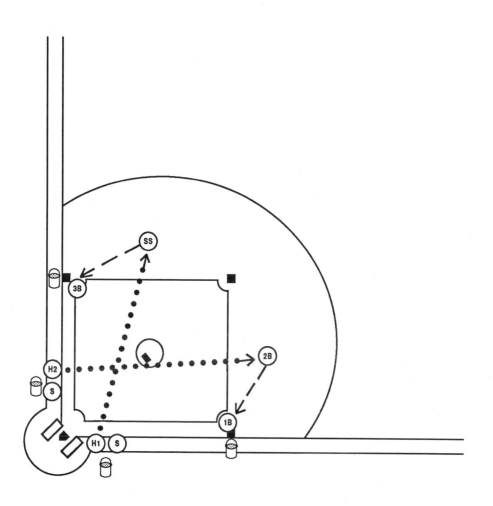

**Second Baseman and Shortstop
Fielding Drill**

Second Baseman and Third Baseman Fielding Drill

Objective:

To provide the second baseman and third baseman with an opportunity to field a large number of ground balls at their positions and to practice throwing accurately to specific bases.

Set-Up:

Drill has two hitters with one on the right side of home plate and the other on the left side of home plate. Both hitters have a shagger. Each shagger stands on the right side of the hitter and has a bucket of balls.

Empty ball buckets are at first and third bases.

The first baseman is at first base, while the second baseman, third baseman, and shortstop are at their defensive positions.

Directions:

Hitter 1 hits a ground ball to the third baseman, who fields the ball and throws it to third base with the shortstop covering the base.

Hitter 2 hits a ground ball to the second baseman, who fields the ball and throws it to first base. Since the drill is designed to provide a large number of ground balls to the second baseman and third baseman, allow the first baseman and shortstop to stay at the bases they are covering for the continuation of the drill. The first baseman and the shortstop then toss the balls into the empty ball buckets.

The manager should maintain a supply of balls to the shaggers.

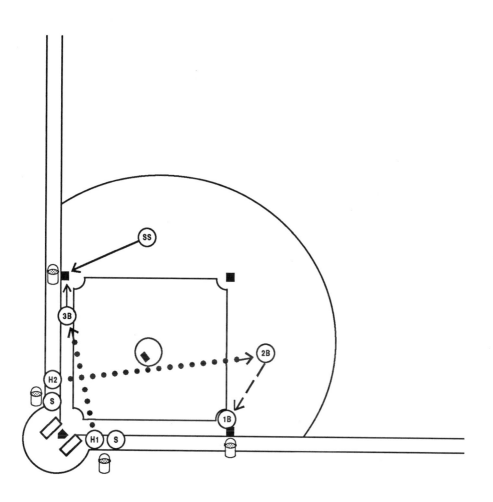

**Second Baseman and Third Baseman
Fielding Drill**

Double Play Drill #1

Objective:

To allow the pitcher, first baseman, and third baseman to practice the timing needed to throw the ball to second base for a double play.

Set-Up:

Drill has one hitter, who is at home plate. (The head coach serves as the hitter.)

The pitcher, catcher, first baseman, second baseman, shortstop, and the third baseman are at their defensive positions.

Directions:

The pitcher pitches a ball to the hitter, who hits to the pitcher, first baseman, or third baseman. If the pitcher or first baseman fields the ball, it is thrown to second base with the shortstop turning the double play. If the third baseman fields the ball, it is thrown to second base with the second baseman turning the double play.

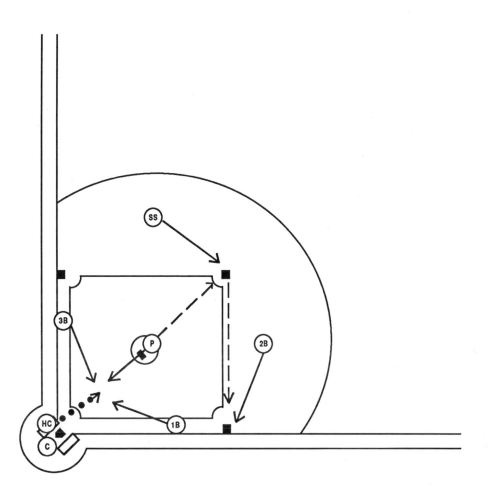

Double Play Drill #1

Double Play Drill #2

Objectives:

1. To improve the infielders' throwing accuracy.
2. To allow the shortstop and second baseman to turn a double play in one drill sequence.

Set-Up:

The first baseman and third baseman are at their respective bases, while the catcher, second baseman, and shortstop are at their defensive positions.

Directions:

The catcher throws the ball to second base with the shortstop turning the double play to first base. The first baseman throws to third base, the third baseman throws to the catcher, the catcher throws back to third base, the third baseman throws to second base with the second baseman turning the double play to first base, and the first baseman throws the ball to the catcher.

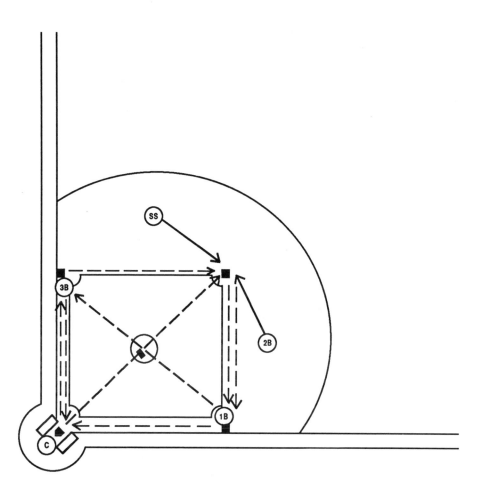

Double Play Drill #2

Double Play Drill #3

Objectives:

1. To improve the infielders' throwing accuracy.
2. To allow the shortstop and second baseman to turn a double play in one drill sequence.

Set-Up:

The first baseman and third baseman are at their respective bases, while the catcher, second baseman, and shortstop are at their defensive positions.

Directions:

The catcher throws the ball to second base with the shortstop turning the double play to first base. The first baseman throws to the catcher, the catcher throws to third base, the third baseman throws to second base with the second baseman turning the double play to first base, and the first baseman throws the ball to the catcher.

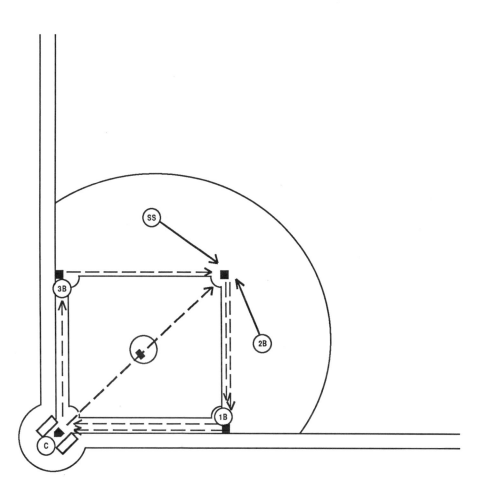

Double Play Drill #3

Combination Drill: Second Baseman Fielding and First Baseman as the Starter for a Double Play

Objectives:

1. To provide the first baseman and second baseman with an opportunity to field a large number of ground balls at their positions and to practice throwing accurately to specific bases.
2. To allow the first baseman to work with the shortstop in turning the double play.

Set-Up:

Drill has two hitters with one on the right side of home plate and the other on the left side of home plate. Both hitters have a shagger. Each shagger stands on the right side of the hitter and has a bucket of balls.

Empty ball buckets are at second and third bases.

The third baseman is at third base, the shortstop is covering second base, and the first baseman and second baseman are at their defensive positions.

Directions:

Hitter 1 hits a ground ball to the second baseman, who fields the ball and throws it to third base.

Hitter 2 hits a ground ball to the first baseman, who fields the ball and throws it to the shortstop. The shortstop practices the pivot for a double play. The shortstop and third baseman then toss the balls into the empty ball buckets.

The manager should maintain a supply of balls to the shaggers.

For safety, it is important that the two hitters alternate hitting.

Variation:

In order to allow the shortstop to make the throw on the double play, have two first basemen, with one at the defensive position and the other at first base.

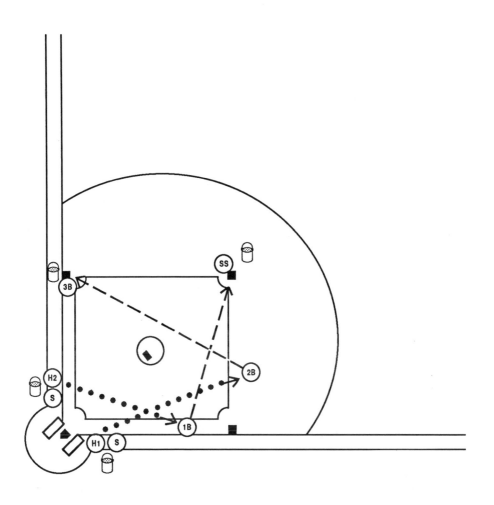

Combination Drill: Second Baseman Fielding and First Baseman as the Starter for a Double Play

Combination Drill: First Baseman Fielding and Second Baseman as the Starter for a Double Play

Objectives:

1. To provide the first baseman and second baseman with an opportunity to field a large number of ground balls at their positions and to practice throwing accurately to specific bases.
2. To allow the second baseman to work with the shortstop in turning the double play.

Set-Up:

Drill has two hitters with one on the right side of home plate and the other on the left side of home plate. Both hitters have a shagger. Each shagger stands on the right side of the hitter and has a bucket of balls.

Empty ball buckets are at second and third bases.

The third baseman is at third base, and the first baseman, second baseman, and shortstop are at their defensive positions.

Directions:

Hitter 1 hits a ground ball to the second baseman, who fields the ball and throws it to the shortstop. The shortstop practices the pivot for a double play.

Hitter 2 hits a ground ball to the first baseman, who fields the ball and throws it to third base. The shortstop and third baseman then toss the balls into the empty ball buckets.

The manager should maintain a supply of balls to the shaggers.

For safety, it is important that the two hitters alternate hitting.

Variation:

In order to allow the shortstop to make the throw on the double play, have two first basemen, with one at the defensive position and the other at first base.

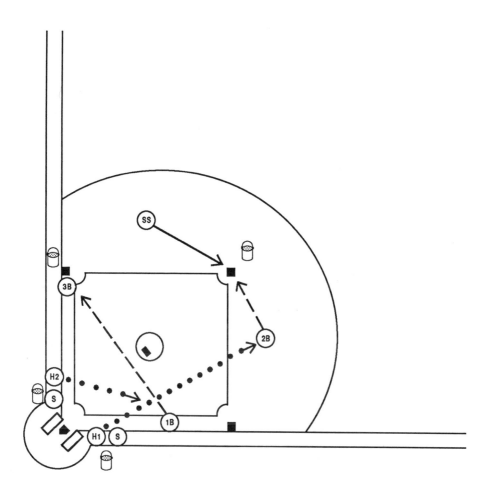

**Combination Drill: First Baseman
Fielding and Second Baseman as the
Starter for a Double Play**

Combination Drill: Third Baseman Fielding and Shortstop as the Starter for a Double Play

Objectives:

1. To provide the third baseman and shortstop with an opportunity to field a large number of ground balls at their positions and to practice throwing accurately to specific bases.
2. To allow the shortstop to work with the second baseman in turning the double play.

Set-Up:

Drill has two hitters with one on the right side of home plate and the other on the left side of home plate. Both hitters have a shagger. Each shagger stands on the right side of the hitter and has a bucket of balls.

Empty ball buckets are at first and second bases.

The first baseman and second baseman are at their respective bases, while the shortstop and third baseman are at their defensive positions.

Directions:

Hitter 1 hits a ground ball to the third baseman, who fields the ball and throws it to first base.

Hitter 2 hits a ground ball to the shortstop, who fields the ball and throws it to second base. The second baseman practices the pivot for a double play. The first baseman and second baseman then toss the balls into the empty ball buckets.

The manager should maintain a supply of balls to the shaggers.

For safety, it is important that the two hitters alternate hitting.

Variation:

In order to allow the second baseman to make the throw on the double play, have two first basemen, with one at first base and the other 6-10 feet directly behind first base.

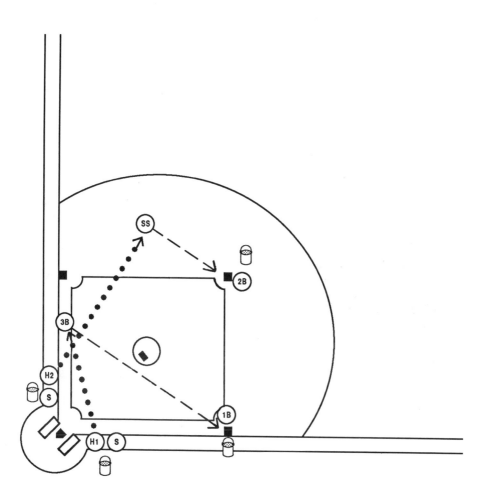

Combination Drill: Third Baseman Fielding and Shortstop as the Starter for a Double Play

Combination Drill: Shortstop Fielding and Third Baseman as the Starter for a Double Play

Objectives:

1. To provide the shortstop and third baseman with an opportunity to field a large number of ground balls at their positions and to practice throwing accurately to specific bases.
2. To allow the third baseman to work with the second baseman in turning the double play.

Set-Up:

Drill has two hitters with one on the right side of home plate and the other on the left side of home plate. Both hitters have a shagger. Each shagger stands on the right side of the hitter and has a bucket of balls.

Empty ball buckets are at first and second bases.

The first baseman and second baseman are at their respective bases, while the shortstop and third baseman are at their defensive positions.

Directions:

Hitter 1 hits a ground ball to the third baseman, who fields the ball and throws it to second base. The second baseman practices the pivot for a double play.

Hitter 2 hits a ground ball to the shortstop, who fields the ball and throws it to first base. The first baseman and second baseman then toss the balls into the empty ball buckets.

The manager should maintain a supply of balls to the shaggers.

For safety, it is important that the two hitters alternate hitting.

Variation:

In order to allow the second baseman to make the throw on the double play, have two first basemen, with one at first base and the other 6-10 feet directly behind first base.

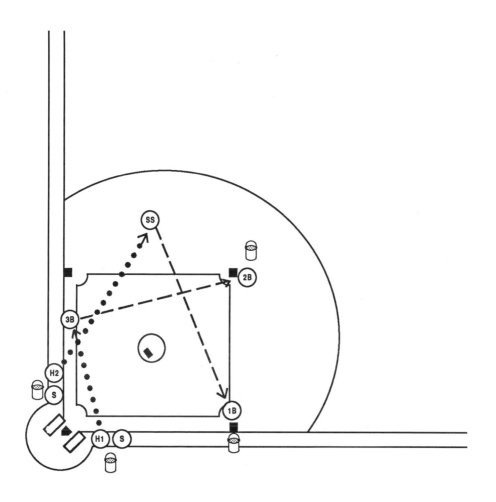

**Combination Drill: Shortstop
Fielding and Third Baseman as the
Starter for a Double Play**

Combination Drill: Second Baseman Fielding and Catcher Preventing Steal at Third Base

Objectives:

1. To provide the second baseman with an opportunity to field the ball while moving to the left and to make accurate throws to first base.
2. To improve the catcher's accuracy in throwing to third base on a steal attempt.

Set-Up:

Drill has one hitter, who is on the left side of home plate, and one shagger, who stands on the right side of the hitter.

Full ball buckets are at home plate and the pitching area.

Empty ball buckets are at first and third bases.

The first baseman is at first base, while the pitcher, catcher, second baseman, shortstop, and third baseman are at their defensive positions.

Directions:

The hitter hits a ground ball to the second baseman's left side. The second baseman fields the ball and throws it to first base. The first baseman tosses the ball into the empty ball bucket.

The pitcher pitches a ball to the catcher, who throws it to third base on an attempted steal. The third baseman moves to the left in order to get out of the way of the throw and the shortstop takes the throw at third base. The shortstop then tosses the ball into the empty ball bucket.

The manager should maintain a supply of balls to the shagger.

For safety, it is important that the hitter and pitcher alternate putting the ball in play.

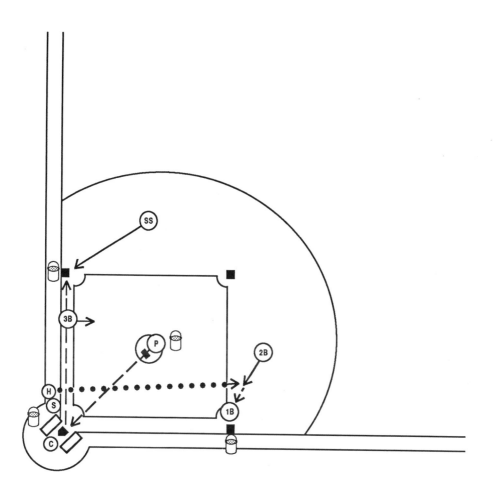

Combination Drill: Second Baseman
Fielding and Catcher Preventing
Steal at Third Base

Combination Drill: Third Baseman Fielding and Catcher Preventing Steal at Second Base

Objectives:

1. To provide the third baseman with an opportunity to field the ball while moving to the left and to make accurate throws to first base.
2. To improve the catcher's accuracy in throwing to second base on a steal attempt.

Set-Up:

Drill has one hitter, who is on the right side of home plate, and one shagger, who stands on the right side of the hitter. Full ball buckets are at home plate and the pitching area.

Empty ball buckets are at first and second bases.

The first baseman is at first base, while the pitcher, catcher, second baseman, shortstop, and third baseman are at their defensive positions.

Directions:

The hitter hits a ground ball to the third baseman's left side. The third baseman fields the ball and throws it to first base. The first baseman tosses the ball into the empty ball bucket.

The pitcher pitches a ball to the catcher, who throws it to second base on an attempted steal. The shortstop takes the throw at second base and the second baseman backs up the throw. The shortstop then tosses the ball into the empty ball bucket.

The manager should maintain a supply of balls to the shagger.

For safety, it is important that the hitter and pitcher alternate putting the ball in play.

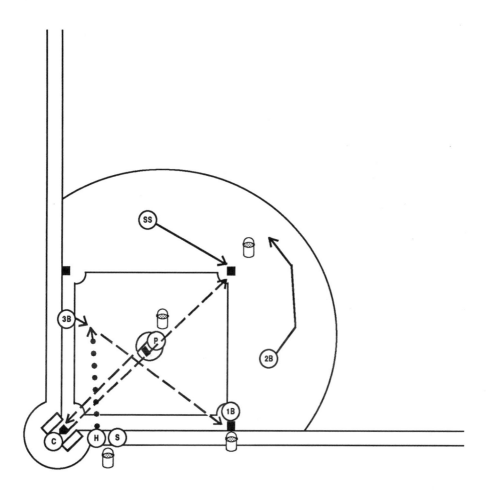

**Combination Drill: Third Baseman
Fielding and Catcher Preventing
Steal at Second Base**

Combination Drill: Shortstop Fielding and Catcher-Second Baseman Preventing a Double Steal

Objectives:

1. To provide the shortstop with an opportunity to field the ball while moving to the right and to make accurate throws to first base.
2. To practice the defense for a double steal.

Set-Up:

Drill has one hitter, who is on the right side of home plate, and one shagger, who stands on the right side of the hitter.

Full ball buckets are at home plate and the pitching area.

Empty ball buckets are at first and third bases.

The first baseman is at first base, while the catcher, pitcher, second baseman, shortstop, and third baseman are at their defensive positions.

Directions:

The hitter hits a ground ball to the shortstop's right side. The shortstop fields the ball and throws it to first base, and the first baseman tosses the ball into the empty ball bucket.

The pitcher pitches a ball to the catcher, who throws it in a direct line toward second base. The second baseman cuts the ball off halfway between the pitching area and second base. The second baseman throws the ball to the third baseman, who has moved to cover third base. Then the third baseman tosses the ball into the empty ball bucket.

The manager should maintain a supply of balls to the shagger.

For safety, it is important that the hitter and pitcher alternate putting the ball in play.

Coaching Hint:

This double steal play is very effective when there is an aggressive runner on third base or a runner who breaks for home as soon as the ball leaves the catcher's hands.

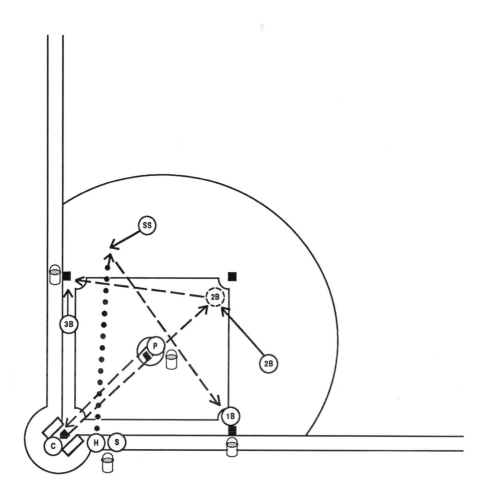

Combination Drill: Shortstop Fielding and Catcher-Second Baseman Preventing a Double Steal

Combination Drill: Fielding Bunts
and Throwing Around the Horn

Objectives:

1. To allow the pitcher, catcher, third baseman, and first baseman to practice fielding bunts and throwing to first base.
2. To improve the infielders' throwing accuracy.

Set-Up:

Drill has one hitter, who is at home plate.

The pitcher, catcher, first baseman, second baseman, shortstop, and the third baseman are at their defensive positions.

Directions:

The pitcher pitches a ball to the hitter who bunts the ball. Then whoever fields the bunt (the catcher, pitcher, first baseman, or third baseman) throws the ball to first base with the second baseman covering the base. The second baseman throws the ball to second base with the shortstop covering the base, and the shortstop throws the ball to third base with either the third baseman or pitcher covering the base. If the third baseman does not field the bunt, then the third baseman covers third base. If the third baseman fields the bunt, then the pitcher covers third base. Whoever covers third base throws the ball back to the catcher. If the drill is to continue, the catcher throws the ball back to the pitcher and the drill begins again.

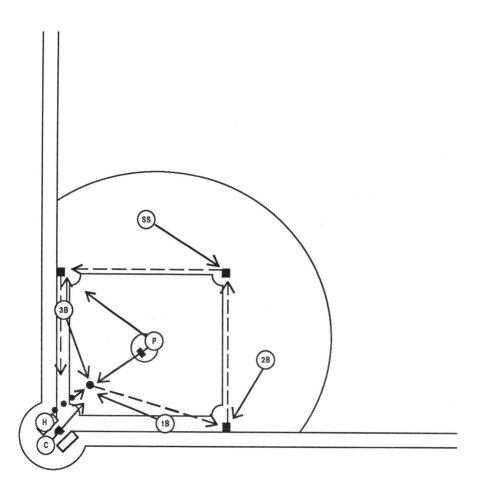

**Combination Drill: Fielding Bunts
and Throwing Around the Horn**

Combination Drill: Double Play with the First Baseman as the Starter and a Bunting Situation with the Shortstop Covering Third Base

Objectives:

1. To allow the first baseman, second baseman, and shortstop to practice working together in turning a double play.
2. To allow the catcher and third baseman to work together in fielding bunts and throwing to third base.

Set-Up:

Drill has one hitter, who is on the left side of home plate, and one shagger, who stands on the right side of the hitter. A tosser is on the right side of home plate.

The shagger and tosser both have full ball buckets.

Empty ball buckets are at first and third bases.

The catcher, first baseman, second baseman, two or more shortstops, and the third baseman are at their defensive positions.

Directions:

The hitter hits a ground ball to the first baseman, who throws to second base with shortstop 1 covering the base and turning the double play. The second baseman covers first base, and after receiving the throw, tosses the ball into the empty ball bucket.

The tosser rolls out a ball similar to a bunted ball, and the catcher and third baseman work together in fielding the ball. The player that fields the ball throws it to third base with shortstop 2 covering the base. Shortstop 2 tosses the ball into the empty ball bucket.

The manager should maintain a supply of balls to the shagger and to the tosser.

For safety, it is important that the hitter and tosser alternate putting the ball in play.

Coaching Hint:

The catcher has priority over the third baseman on a bunted ball that is to be thrown to third base.

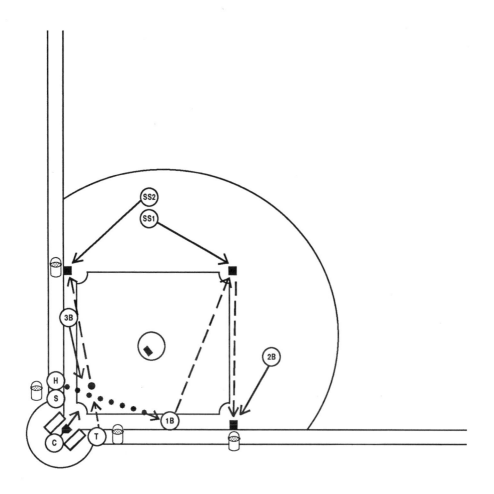

**Combination Drill: Double Play
with the First Baseman as the Starter
and a Bunting Situation with the
Shortstop Covering Third Base**

From using the drills contained in this chapter, your infielders should improve on the following:

1. Throwing accuracy
2. Performing fundamentals in playing positions
3. Turning double plays
4. Covering of bases and tags
5. Preventing steal attempts

4

Outfielders' Drills

Drills for improving the following outfielders' skills are presented in this chapter:
1. Locating the outfield fence while playing a deep fly ball
2. Communicating with other players when attempting to field or catch the same ball
3. Catching a low, dropping ball that is hit in front of the outfielder
4. Performing the one hop-step throw
5. Fielding a ground ball and quickly throwing it to a specific base
6. Moving up and back to catch fly balls
7. Catching difficultly hit balls
8. Working with other players after a difficult catch

Outfield Fence Drill

Objective:

To allow the outfielders to practice locating the outfield fence in order to overcome the fear of running into the fence while playing a deep fly ball.

Set-Up:

Drill has three tossers, who each have a shagger standing on the right side of them.

Drill has one or more outfielders in each outfield position.

The outfielders are at their defensive positions.

Directions:

The first outfielder in each line runs back toward the fence and locates the fence by touching it. At the same time, the tosser throws a fly ball just short of the fence causing the player to have to come back to catch the ball. The outfielder then returns the ball to the respective shagger.

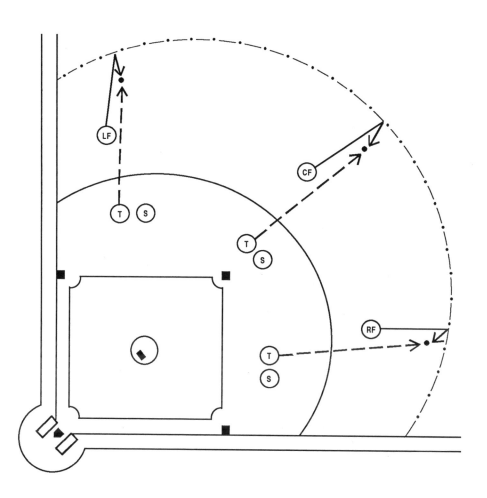

Outfield Fence Drill

Infield/Outfield Jurisdiction Drill #1

Objective:

To improve communication among players when attempting to field or catch the same ball.

Set-Up:

Drill has two tossers, who are in front of home plate. Each tosser has a shagger, who stands on the right side of the tosser.

Drill has one or more players at the defensive positions for the first baseman, second baseman, shortstop, third baseman, right fielder, and left fielder.

Directions:

Tosser 1 throws a fly ball deep in the gap behind first base, while tosser 2 throws a fly ball deep in the gap behind third base. The first baseman, second baseman, and right fielder work together to catch the fly ball thrown by tosser 1, while the shortstop, third baseman, and left fielder work together to catch the fly ball thrown by tosser 2.

The outfielders have jurisdiction over all infielders. Therefore, if an outfielder calls for the fly ball, the infielders should allow the outfielder to field the ball.

Coaching Hint:

At the beginning of the season, it is important for you to establish a fly ball jurisdiction rule.

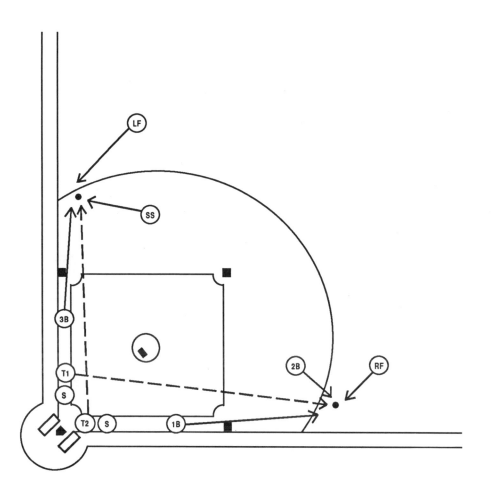

Infield/Outfield Jurisdiction Drill #1

Infield/Outfield Jurisdiction Drill #2

Objective:

To improve communication among players when attempting to field or catch the same ball.

Set-Up:

Drill has one tosser, who is in front of the pitching area, and a shagger, who stands on the right side of the tosser.

Drill has one or more players at the defensive positions for the second baseman, shortstop, and center fielder.

Directions:

The tosser throws a fly ball behind second base. The second baseman, shortstop, and center fielder work together to catch the fly ball.

The outfielders have jurisdiction over all infielders. Therefore, if an outfielder calls for the fly ball, the infielders should allow the outfielder to field the ball.

Coaching Hint:

At the beginning of the season, it is important for you to establish a fly ball jurisdiction rule.

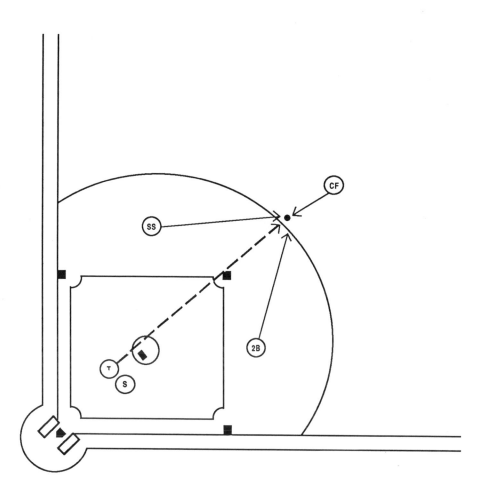

Infield/Outfield Jurisdiction Drill #2

Slide and Catch Drill

Objective:

To improve the outfielder's ability to catch a low, dropping ball that is hit in front of the outfielder.

Set-Up:

The outfielders are divided into two groups. Each group is arranged in a line about 90 feet in front of a hitter.

The drill has two hitters, with one hitter on the right field sideline and the other hitter on the left field sideline. Each hitter has a shagger, who stands on the right side of the hitter.

Directions:

The hitter hits a fly ball in front of the outfielder.

The outfielder performs a bent-leg slide while catching the ball and then throws the ball to the respective shagger.

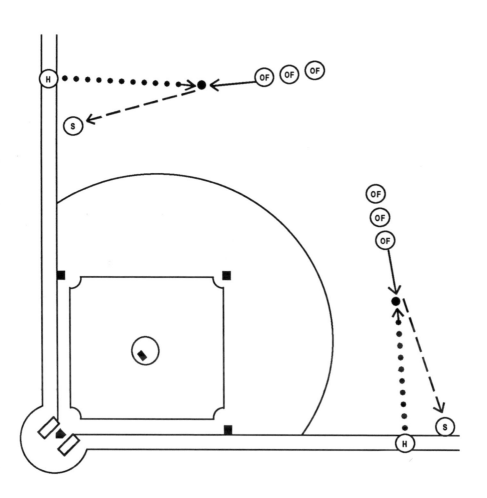

Slide and Catch Drill

Hop-Step Throw Drill

Objective:

To improve the one hop-step throw.

Set-Up:

The outfielders are divided into partners, who are 100 feet apart.

Directions:

The partners move at the same time to field an imaginary ball that is hit in front of them. After fielding the ball, they perform the one hop-step throw making sure to use a complete follow-through. Then the partners exchange places, and the drill continues for as long as desired.

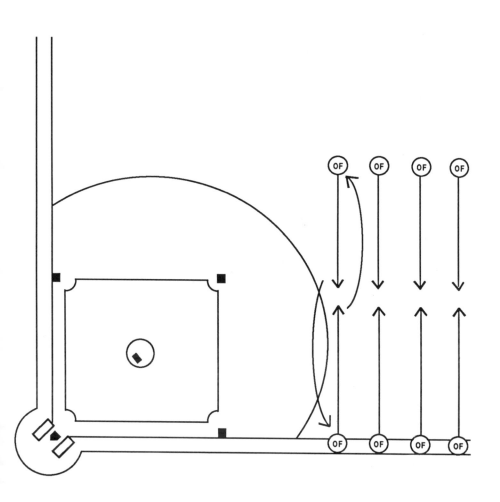

Hop-Step Throw Drill

Quick Throw Drill

Objective:

To improve the outfielder's ability to field a ground ball and quickly throw it to a base.

Set-Up:

Drill has three tossers and three shaggers. Each tosser is near a base and has a shagger, who is at the base.

Drill has one or more outfielders at each of the outfield defensive positions. The outfielders are pulled up in order to get a force play at a base.

Directions:

The tosser throws a ground ball to the outfielder, who fields the ball and quickly throws it to the respective shagger.

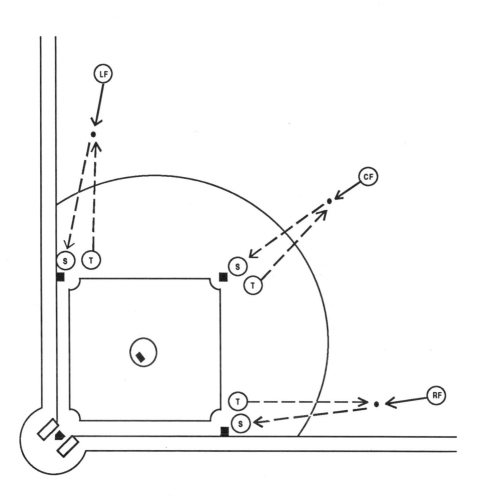

Quick Throw Drill

Weave Drill

Objective:

To improve the outfielder's ability to move up and back to catch fly balls.

Set-Up:

All outfielders start in a line in deep left field. The head coach is in front of the left field grass area, the assistant coach is in front of the center field grass area, and the manager is in front of the right field grass area.

Directions:

The head coach throws a short fly ball to the outfielder, making the outfielder move up. The outfielder throws the ball back to the head coach and then runs toward center field, where the head coach leads the outfielder with the ball. After catching the ball, the outfielder throws it to the assistant coach, and the assistant coach and the manager repeat the same drill sequence with the outfielder. After the manager has completed the sequence, the drill is reversed and performed in the opposite direction, so the outfielder finishes the drill in left field.

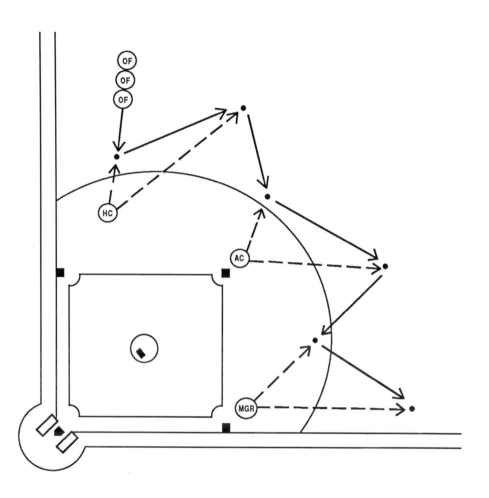

Weave Drill

Outfielders' Flip Drill

Objectives:

1. To improve the player's ability to catch a difficultly hit ball.
2. To improve the ability of players to work together after a difficult catch.

Set-Up:

Drill has one hitter, who is in the baseline between second and third bases.

Drill has one shagger, who is at second base.

Drill has two or more outfielders in a line at the center fielder's defensive position and the left fielder's defensive position.

Directions:

The hitter hits a ground ball to the center fielder's non-glove side, causing the center fielder to field the ball backhanded. The center fielder flips the ball to the left fielder, who throws the ball to the shagger. The outfielders go to the ends of the opposite lines.

Variations:

1. The shagger is at third base. The left fielder fields the ball on the glove hand side and flips the ball to the center fielder, who throws the ball to third base.

2. The center fielder fields the ball on the glove hand side and flips the ball to the right fielder, who throws the ball to second or third base.

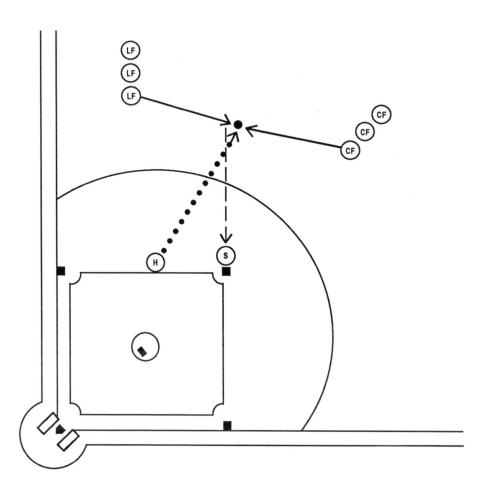

Outfielders' Flip Drill

Outfielders' Throwing Drill

Objective:

To allow the outfielders to practice fielding a large number of ground balls and to practice throwing the balls to specific bases.

Set-Up for Rounds 1 and 2:

Drill has one or more outfielders at each of the outfield defensive positions.

Hitter 1 is near first base with a shagger at first base. Hitter 2 is near second base with a shagger at second base. Hitter 3 is near third base with a shagger at third base.

Each hitter has a full ball bucket.

Directions for Round 1:

Hitter 1 hits a ground ball to the center fielder, who throws to first base. Hitter 2 hits a ground ball to the right fielder, who throws to second base. Hitter 3 hits a ground ball to the left fielder, who throws to third base. After 5 minutes, the players begin round 2.

Directions for Round 2:

Hitter 1 hits a ground ball to the right fielder, who throws to first base. Hitter 2 hits a ground ball to the left fielder, who throws to second base. Hitter 3 hits a ground ball to the center fielder, who throws to third base. After 5 minutes, the players begin round 3.

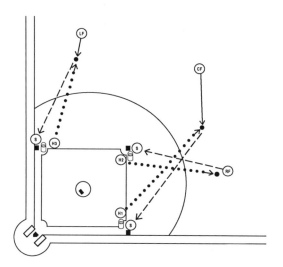

Round 1

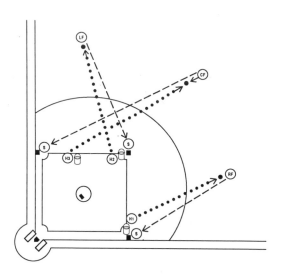

Round 2

Outfielders' Throwing Drill

Outfielders' Throwing Drill
(Continued)

Set-Up for Round 3:

Drill has one or more outfielders at each of the outfield defensive positions.

Hitter 1 is halfway between the pitching area and second base with a shagger at third base. Hitter 2 is near second base with a shagger at second base. Hitter 3 is to the left of the pitching area with a shagger at the cutoff position.

Each hitter has a full ball bucket.

Directions for Round 3:

Hitter 1 hits a ground ball to the right fielder, who throws to third base. Hitter 2 hits a ground ball to the center fielder, who throws to second base. Hitter 3 hits a ground ball to the left fielder, who throws to the cutoff person.

NOTE: THIS IS AN EXCELLENT DRILL IN ORDER FOR THE OUTFIELDERS TO GET A LOT OF PRACTICE ON FIELDING AND THROWING IN A SHORT PERIOD OF TIME. HOWEVER, FOR SAFETY, IT IS IMPORTANT THAT THE HITTERS AND SHAGGERS BE AWARE OF EACH OTHER'S POSITIONS, AND THAT THE OUTFIELDERS PAY ATTENTION TO WHERE THEY ARE THROWING THE BALLS.

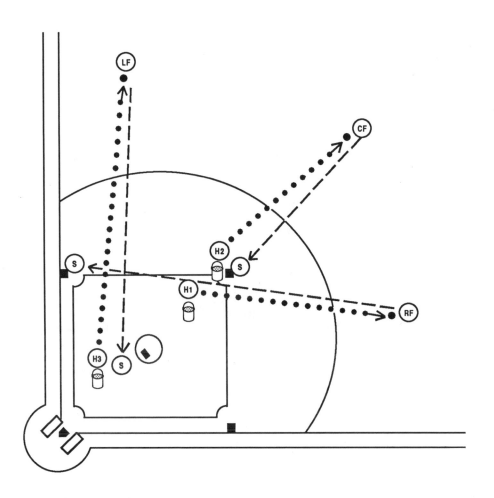

Round 3

Outfielders' Throwing Drill

Outfielders' Communication Drill

Objective:

To improve the outfielder's ability to use teamwork when fielding balls that have been hit between two outfielders.

Set-Up:

Drill has two hitters, with one hitter on the right side of home plate, and the other hitter on the left side of home plate. Each hitter has a batting tee and a full ball bucket.

A protective screen is at second base with the manager behind it. The manager has an empty ball bucket.

Drill has two or more outfielders at each of the outfield defensive positions.

Directions:

Hitter 1 hits a ball between the left fielder and the center fielder. One outfielder calls for the ball, and the other outfielder moves into position to back up the fielder. The fielder throws the ball to second base.

Hitter 2 hits a ball between the right fielder and the center fielder. One outfielder calls for the ball, and the other outfielder moves into position to back up the fielder. The fielder throws the ball to second base.

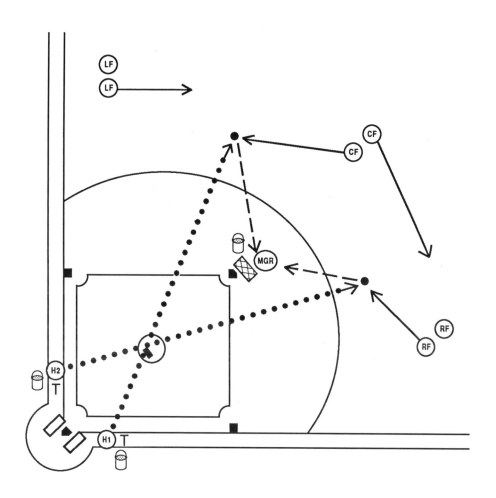

Outfielders' Communication Drill

From using the drills contained in this chapter, your outfielders should improve on the following:

1. Locating the outfield fence in order to overcome the fear of running into the fence while playing a deep fly ball
2. Communicating with other players when attempting to field or catch the same ball
3. Catching a low, dropping ball that is hit in front of them
4. Performing the one hop-step throw
5. Fielding a ground ball and quickly throwing it to a specific base
6. Moving up and back to catch fly balls
7. Catching difficultly hit balls
8. Working together with other players after a difficult catch

Pitching Programs and Drills

The following programs for a pitcher are presented in this chapter:
1. Stretching
2. Weekly practice
3. Pre-game warm-up

Also, drills for improving the following pitcher's skills are presented in this chapter:
1. Catching a hard hit line drive
2. Reacting in a lateral direction for catching a ball
3. Reacting and moving laterally in fielding a ground ball
4. Fielding bunts
5. Executing the bunt defense with a runner at third base

Stretching Program

Stretching is an important aspect of the pitcher's training program. A good stretching program should increase flexibility and strength of the wrist, elbow, and shoulder of the pitching arm. Whenever a pitcher does not utilize a stretching program prior to pitching, the pitcher places strenuous demands on the pitching arm and is prone to being injured. The following is a sample stretching program that should be used prior to pitching activities.

A. Jog ½ mile

B. Arm Circles and Stretch
Move pitching arm in a full circle. Stretch the hand as far out as possible throughout the action. Alternate forward circles and backward circles (simulate the windmill circle, not a small circle.) Movement should be at medium speed with a relaxed stretching effort.
Repetitions: 4 sets of 10 repetitions with 15 seconds rest between sets.

C. Speed Circles
Move pitching arm in a full circle using a windmill motion at maximum speed.
Repetitions: 4 sets of 10 repetitions with 30 seconds rest between sets.

D. Resistance Pitching
Place the palms of the hands on each end of the softball bat. With the right arm in a slingshot pitching position, at the height of the backswing, move the arm from as far back as possible to the point of release, while resisting as strongly as possible with the left hand palm pushing the bat into the pitching hand palm. Use maximum effort!

E. Shoulder/Arm Relaxation
Repeat "B" to release tension. 10 repetitions only.

F. Wrist Snap
Hold a book or other weight at the release position and snap the wrist back and forth as far and as fast as possible, until fatigued. Then move the wrist in circles until tired, alternating the direction for each set, backwards and forwards.
Repetitions: 4 sets to fatigue with 30 seconds rest between sets.

G. Arm Lifts and Relax

Lift the arms out sideways and up overhead, while raising the chest high. Let the arms drop loosely to the sides, the head fall forward onto the chest, and relax the knees. Use before the game and between innings to control tension.

Repetitions: 10 repetitions with no rest between repetitions.

H. Hand Strength/Forearm Strength

Use V-shaped hand dynomometer. Hold in second joint of thumb and first joint (from top) of fingers. Squeeze through the complete range of motion 10 times as quickly as possible.

Repetitions: 5 sets with 10 seconds rest between sets.

I. Jog ½ mile.

Weekly Practice Program

Pitchers, like other players on the team, must have well-planned practice schedules in order to meet both daily and long-range goals. The practice schedules should be designed to gradually strengthen the pitching arm throughout the season and to meet the needs of the individual pitcher. The following is a sample pitcher's weekly practice program, which alternates speed work with endurance work.

Weekly Practice Program
(Early season)

Monday	Tuesday	Wednesday	Thursday	Friday	Notes
1. Jog ½ mile 2. Stretch 3. Arm circles and stretch (4 x 10) 4. Speed circles (4 x 10) 5. Resistance pitching (4 x 6) 6. Repeat #3 7. Arm lifts and relax (10) 8. Throw ball against fence (working hip rotation) (15) 9. 15 x 10 yard sprints 0. Wrist snap (4 x fatigue) 1. 40 style pitches 2. 3 x 10 speed pitches 3. 4 x 10 corner pitches 4. 5 x 10 different pitches 5. Style/relaxation (10 style pitches, 5 speed pitches) 6. Repeat #3	1-10. Same 11. 50 style pitches 12. 30 rise pitches 13. 30 drop pitches 14. 4 x 10 (alternate rise and drop pitches) 15. 4 x 10 (alternate drop pitches) 16. 2 x 10 (alternate rise and change pitches) 17. 25 style pitches 18. Jog ¼ mile	1-10. Same 11. 30 style pitches 12. 4 x 10 speed pitches (rest between pitches 13. 30 style pitches 14. 3 x 10 speed pitches (no rest between repetitions) 15. 25 style pitches 16. 2 x 10 speed pitches (rest between pitches 17. Pitch four innings with catcher 18. Jog ¼ mile	1-10. Same 11. Pitch batting practice 10 mins on/ 5 mins off Total 90 mins 12. Jog 1 mile	Same as Wednesday	

Pre-Game Warm-Up Program

The pre-game warm-up program is an extremely important phase of pitching. It allows the pitcher to properly warm-up the pitching arm so there is less chance of injury. Also, it allows the pitcher to work on the mechanics of each type of pitch and to correct any faults prior to the game. Plus, it gives the pitcher a sense of confidence in starting the game in control of the situation. The following is a sample pitcher's pre-game warm-up program, which should vary depending on the needs of the pitcher.

1. Team's stretching program
2. Jog ½ mile
3. 2 x 150 feet   striding
   2 x 150 feet   high knee running/jogging (75 feet each)
   2 x 150 feet   alternating speed
   4 x 60 feet   sprinting
4. Pitcher's stretching program
5. 25 wrist snaps
6. 20 drop pitches
7. 20 rise pitches
8. 20 change pitches
9. 2 x 10 speed pitches
10. 10-20 various pitches
11. Go over signals with catcher
12. 3 x 60 feet   sprinting at ¾ speed

Line Drive Drill

Objective:

To improve the pitcher's ability to catch a hard hit line drive and throw to specific bases.

Set-Up:

Pitcher 1, catcher, shortstop, and third baseman are at their defensive positions, while pitcher 2 is on the first base sideline.

The head coach serves as the hitter and is at home plate.

The head coach has a full ball bucket, and the catcher has an empty ball bucket.

Directions:

Pitcher 1 pitches a ball. As the ball gets to the catcher, the head coach hits another ball as a line drive to pitcher 1, who catches the ball and throws the ball to second base.

The drill sequence is then repeated with pitcher 1 throwing the ball to third base.

After eight repetitions, the pitchers rotate positions. The drill continues for as long as desired.

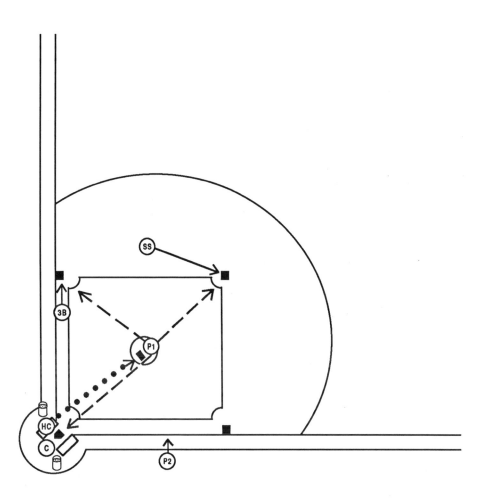

Line Drive Drill

Lateral Reaction Drill

Objective:

To improve the pitcher's ability to react in a lateral direction for catching a ball.

Set-Up:

Pitcher 1 is at the defensive position.
Pitcher 2 is 20 feet in front of pitcher 1 and has a full ball bucket.

Directions:

Pitcher 1 simulates a pitch. Then pitcher 2 throws a ball randomly to the right or left of pitcher 1 making pitcher 1 reach to catch the ball.

After eight repetitions, the pitchers rotate positions. The drill continues for as long as desired.

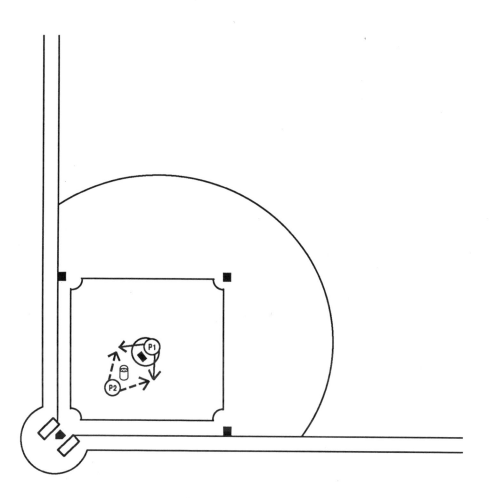

Lateral Reaction Drill

Pitcher's Lateral Movement Drill

Objective:

To improve the pitcher's ability to react and move laterally in fielding a ground ball and to practice throwing to first base.

Set-Up:

Pitcher 1 is at the defensive position, while pitcher 2 is behind the pitching area.

The catcher and first baseman are at their defensive positions. The head coach serves as the hitter and is at home plate.

Directions:

Pitcher 1 pitches a ball. As the ball gets to the catcher, the head coach hits another ball to the right or left of pitcher 1, who fields the ball and throws it to first base.

The pitchers rotate positions, and the drill sequence is repeated. The drill continues for as long as desired.

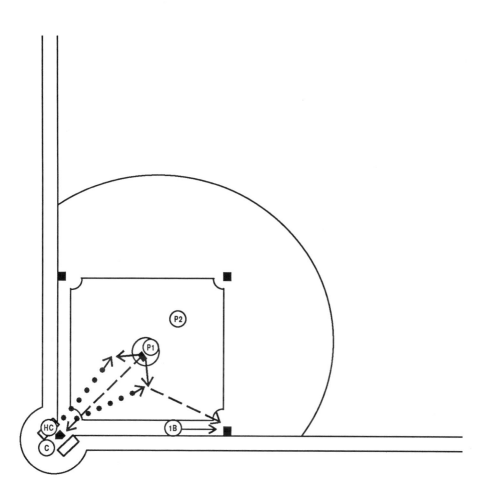

Pitcher's Lateral Movement Drill

Fielding Bunts Drill

Objective:

To improve the pitcher's ability to field bunts and throw to specific bases.

Set-Up:

There are two or more pitchers in the pitching area.

The first baseman and third baseman are at their respective bases, while the shortstop is at second base.

The head coach is in the vicinity of home plate and has a full ball bucket.

Four balls are placed in front of home plate.

Directions:

Pitcher 1 simulates a pitch, fields a bunt, and throws the ball to first base. Pitcher 2 simulates a pitch, fields a bunt, and throws the ball to first base. The pitchers continue to rotate and perform in the same manner while throwing the balls to second and third bases.

The head coach keeps a supply of balls in front of home plate.

The drill continues for as long as desired.

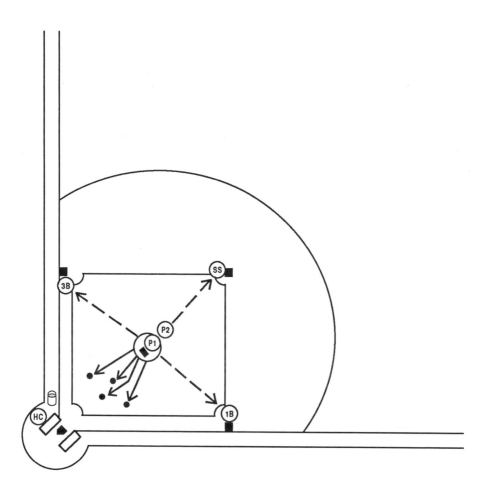

Fielding Bunts Drill

Pitcher's Bunt Defense with
a Runner at Third Base Drill

Objective:

To improve the pitcher's ability to execute the bunt defense with a runner at third base.

Set-Up:

Pitcher 1 and the catcher are at their defensive positions, while pitcher 2 is behind the pitching area.

Three or more runners are at third base.

The head coach serves as the hitter and is at home plate.

Directions:

Pitcher 1 pitches a ball, and the head coach bunts the ball. Pitcher 1 fields the bunt and throws the ball to home plate to get out the runner, who has tried to advance home on a squeeze play.

The pitchers rotate positions, and the drill sequence is repeated.

The drill continues for as long as desired.

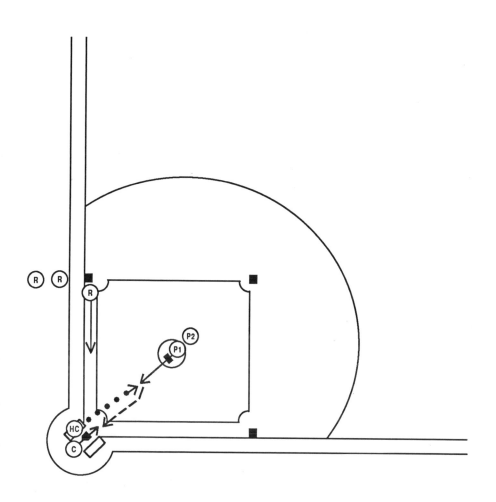

**Pitcher's Bunt Defense with
a Runner at Third Base Drill**

From using the programs and drills contained in this chapter, your pitcher should improve on the following:

1. Increasing flexibility and strength of the wrist, elbow, and shoulder of the pitching arm
2. Properly warming-up prior to a game
3. Catching a hard hit line drive
4. Reacting in a lateral direction for catching a ball
5. Reacting and moving laterally in fielding a ground ball
6. Fielding bunts
7. Executing the bunt defense with a runner at third base

6

Catching Drills

Drills for improving the following skills of a catcher are presented in this chapter:
1. Positioning the glove
2. Framing pitches
3. Catching corner pitches
4. Blocking wild pitches
5. Fielding bunts
6. Communicating with other infielders on catching fly balls
7. Quickly taking the ball out of the glove
8. Quickly releasing the ball on throws
9. Throwing out runners on steal attempts
10. Catching throws from the infield and outfield
11. Making tag plays at home plate
12. Communicating with the cut-off person on throws from the outfield

Also, there are drills for strengthening the arms and shoulders for throwing.

Section 1

Set-Up for Drills in Section 1:

Drills should be performed by two catchers at home plate, if possible.

For some drills, you might want to use your pitcher or a pitching machine instead of catcher 1.

Catcher 2 is located in the defensive position.

If catcher 1 or a pitcher is used, have them start the drills with a full bucket of balls to conserve time. Then catcher 2 can place the caught balls in an empty bucket. This will prevent catcher 2 from having to throw the balls back to catcher 1 at the end of the drills.

NOTE: FULL PROTECTIVE CATCHING GEAR SHOULD BE WORN BY THE CATCHER WHEN IN THE DEFENSIVE POSITION, UNLESS OTHERWISE STATED IN THE DIRECTIONS FOR THE DRILL.

Catcher's One-Knee Throwing Drill

Objective:

To improve arm and shoulder strength for throwing.

Directions:

The catchers kneel 30 feet apart on their left knees. After throwing the ball back and forth for a designated time period, they move apart 10 more feet. The drill continues until the throws equal the distance from home plate to second base.

Catcher's Two-Knee Throwing Drill

Objectives:

1. To improve arm and shoulder strength for throwing.
2. To practice throwing the ball overhand.

Directions:

The catchers kneel 30 feet apart on both knees. After throwing the ball back and forth for a designated time period, they move apart 10 more feet. The drill continues for as long as desired. Also, the catchers should emphasize throwing the ball overhand.

Soft Hands Drill

Objective:

To improve relaxation of the hands, which aids in developing the soft hands necessary for receiving the ball properly.

Directions:

Catcher 1 throws tennis balls from 20-30 feet away to catcher 2. Catcher 2 practices giving with the hands when catching the ball.

NOTE: THE ONLY CATCHING GEAR NEEDED FOR THIS DRILL IS THE FACE MASK.

Quick Hands Drill

Objective:

To improve the quickness of the catcher's hands.

Directions:

Catcher 1 throws the ball hard from 20-30 feet away to catcher 2. The balls are thrown high, low, inside, and outside of home plate. If a pitching machine is available, it can be used for this drill.

Quick Feet Drill

Objective:

To improve the quickness of the catcher's feet when balls are pitched to the inside and outside of home plate.

Directions:

Catcher 1 throws the ball hard from 20-30 feet away to catcher 2. Catcher 2 takes a jab step to the left or right attempting to get the middle of the body in front of the ball. If a pitching machine is available, it can be used for this drill.

Quick Release Drill

Objectives:

1. To improve the catcher's quickness in taking the ball out of the glove.
2. To improve footwork and to practice quickly releasing a throw.

Directions:

The catchers, who are 60-70 feet apart, throw to each other playing "hard catch." They work on taking the ball out of the glove quickly and on utilizing proper footwork while emphasizing quick releases on the throws.

Glove Roll Drill

Objective:

To improve the technique of rolling the glove, so the glove is in the best position for reacting to the ball.

Directions:

Catcher 1 throws the ball from 20-30 feet away to catcher 2. As the thrown ball is released, catcher 2 moves the glove one-quarter of a turn to the left, so that the glove is parallel to the ground. The glove is now halfway between a palms-up catch and a fingers-up catch. From this position, the catcher can make the best decision for catching the ball.

Framing Drill

Objective:

To improve the catcher's ability to frame pitches and to shift the body weight for pitches that are slightly outside the width of the shoulders.

Directions:

Catcher 1 stands in front of catcher 2 and uses a ball on a stick to simulate pitches that are high, low, inside, and outside of home plate. Catcher 2 practices framing the pitches and shifting the body weight for pitches that are slightly outside the width of the shoulders.

Sway and Frame Drill

Objectives:

1. To improve the technique of catching the outside of the ball on inside and outside corner pitches.
2. To improve the technique of catching high and low pitches.

Directions:

Catcher 1 throws the ball from 20-30 feet away and throws it slightly outside of catcher 2's shoulders, thereby requiring catcher 2 to use a sway shift to catch the ball correctly.

No Hands Drill

Objective:

To improve foot and body mechanics for blocking balls that are pitched into the dirt.

Directions:

Catcher 1 throws the ball from 20-30 feet away to catcher 2. Catcher 2 has both hands placed behind the back, with the head down and the shoulders rounded. Catcher 2 concentrates on keeping the ball in front of the body.

NOTE: ALL PROTECTIVE CATCHING GEAR, EXCEPT THE GLOVE, SHOULD BE WORN WHEN IN THE DEFENSIVE POSITION FOR THIS DRILL.

Blocking Drill

Objective:

To improve the technique of blocking wild pitches thrown to the left, right, and in front of home plate.

Directions:

Catcher 1 throws wild pitches from 20-30 feet away to catcher 2. Catcher 2 practices blocking the wild pitches. If a pitching machine is available, it can be used for this drill.

NOTE: FULL PROTECTIVE CATCHING GEAR SHOULD BE WORN BY THE CATCHER, PLUS SPECIAL PROTECTION IS RECOMMENDED FOR THIS DRILL. THE CATCHER'S ARMS SHOULD BE PADDED WITH KNEE PADS.

Foul Ball Drill

Objective:

To improve the technique of catching foul balls.

Directions:

Catcher 1 throws foul balls in the vicinity of home plate to catcher 2. Catcher 2 practices locating and catching the foul balls.

Section 2

Foul Ball Communication Drill

Objective:

To improve communication between the catcher, pitcher, first baseman, and third baseman on the location of foul balls.

Set-Up:

The catcher, pitcher, first baseman, and third baseman are at their defensive positions.

The head coach is behind the catcher at home plate.

Directions:

The head coach throws a foul ball in the direction of first base, third base, or the middle. The infielders visualize home plate as being divided into the following three areas:

If the foul ball goes to the third base side, behind or in front of home plate, the infielders call, "up 3", which lets the catcher know to turn to the third base side. It is the responsibility of the defensive player on the foul ball side to call the play. For example, if the ball goes to the third base side of home plate, the third baseman should call "up 3"

NOTE: FULL PROTECTIVE CATCHING GEAR SHOULD BE WORN BY THE CATCHER FOR THIS DRILL.

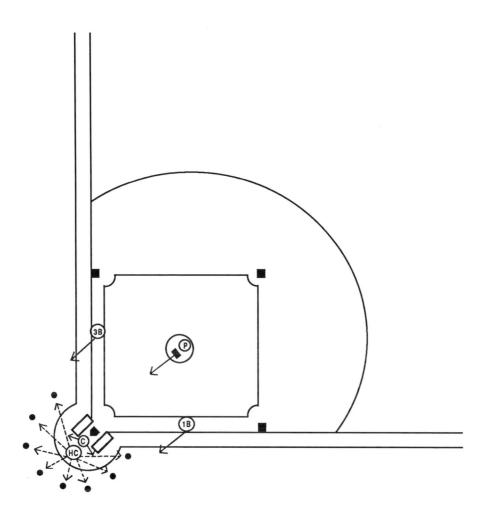

Foul Ball Communication Drill

Pop Fly Communication Drill

Objective:

To improve the pop fly communication between the catcher, pitcher, first baseman, and third baseman.

Set-Up:

The catcher, pitcher, first baseman, and third baseman are at their defensive positions.

The head coach is behind the catcher at home plate.

Directions:

The head coach throws a pop fly between the four infielders' positions, and the infielders work together in calling for the pop fly. At the beginning of the season, it is important for you to establish a fly ball jurisdiction rule. For example, the first baseman would have jurisdiction over the pitcher, etc.

NOTE: FULL PROTECTIVE CATCHING GEAR SHOULD BE WORN BY THE CATCHER FOR THIS DRILL.

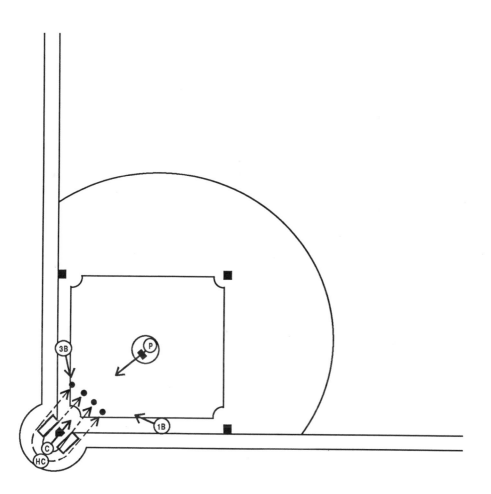

Pop Fly Communication Drill

Catcher's Fielding Bunts Drill

Objective:

To improve the catcher's ability to field bunts and throw to specific bases.

Set-Up:

If you have four catchers, place one at each base. If you have three or fewer catchers, then you will need to use additional players at the bases, and let the catchers alternate in practicing the drill.

Six balls are placed in front of home plate.

Catcher 1 is in the defensive position.

Directions:

When ready, catcher 1 pops-up, fields the bunt, and throws in the following sequence: to first base, to second base, and to third base while returning to the defensive position between throws. The drill continues until catcher 1 has thrown two balls to each base. The players then rotate counter-clockwise.

NOTE: FULL PROTECTIVE CATCHING GEAR SHOULD BE WORN BY THE CATCHER WHEN IN THE DEFENSIVE POSITION.

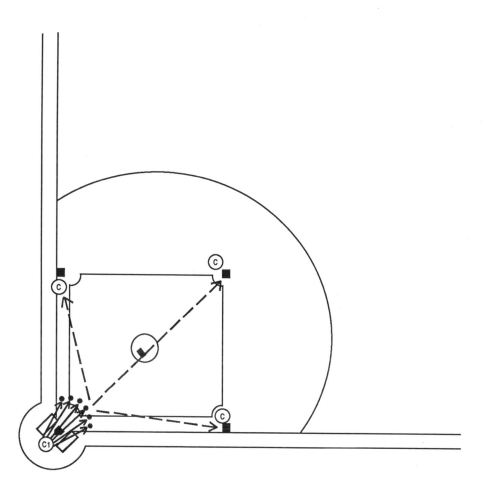

Catcher's Fielding Bunts Drill

Steal Attempts Drill

Objective:

To improve the catcher's ability to throw out runners on steal attempts.

Set-Up:

Drill has three to four runners at first and second bases.

There are two or more catchers, second basemen, and shortstops at their defensive positions.

Directions:

The pitcher pitches a ball to the catcher. On the release of the pitch, the first runner at first base breaks to second base on a steal attempt. Catcher 1 attempts to throw the runner out. On the release of the next pitch, the first runner at second base breaks to third base on a steal attempt and catcher 1 attempts to throw that runner out. The catchers then rotate.

The two shortstops alternate taking the throws at second and third bases.

NOTE: FULL PROTECTIVE CATCHING GEAR SHOULD BE WORN BY THE CATCHER WHEN IN THE DEFENSIVE POSITION.

Variation:

It is understood that in some defensive systems, the second baseman takes the throw at second base on a steal attempt. Therefore, the second baseman can practice taking the throw at second base.

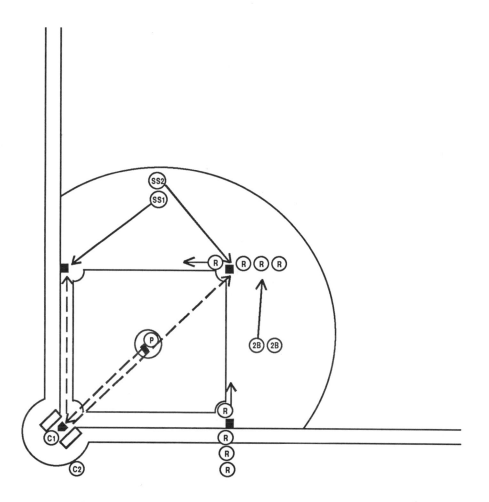

Steal Attempts Drill

Force Play at Home Drill

Objective:

To improve the catcher's ability to catch throws from the infield and make throws to first base.

Set-Up:

Drill has one hitter, who is at home plate. (The head coach serves as the hitter.)

The catcher, first baseman, second baseman, third baseman, and shortstop are at their defensive positions.

A full ball bucket is at home plate.

An empty ball bucket is at first base.

Directions:

The hitter hits a ball to the third baseman, who fields the ball and throws it to home plate. The catcher touches home plate for a forced play and throws the ball to first base for the second out.

The drill continues in the same manner with the hitter hitting a ball to the shortstop, to the second baseman, and then to the first baseman.

On balls hit to the first baseman, the second baseman will need to cover first base for the second out, since the first baseman will not have time to get back to the base.

NOTE: FULL PROTECTIVE CATCHING GEAR SHOULD BE WORN BY THE CATCHER. IT IS UNDERSTOOD THAT DURING THE GAME THERE ARE TIMES THAT THE FACE MASK WILL BE REMOVED AND THROWN OUT OF THE LINE OF PLAY.

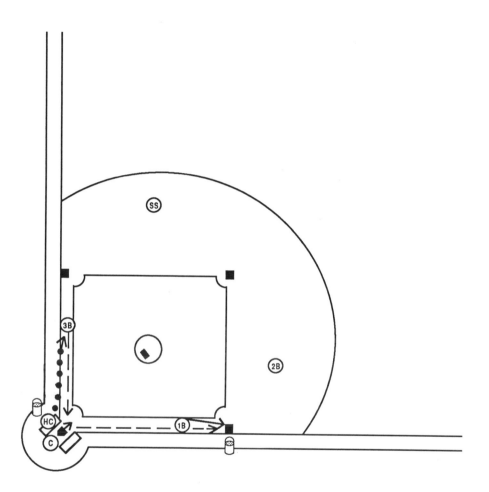

Force Play at Home Drill

Tag Play Drill

Objective:

To improve the catcher's ability to catch throws from the outfield and make tag plays at home plate.

Set-Up:

The catchers are at home plate.

Three to six outfielders are at the edge of the outfield grass. The outfielders have 3 balls each.

Directions:

Outfielder 1 starts by rolling a ball a few feet out in front, picking up the ball, and making a strong throw to home plate. After catching the ball, the catcher simulates a tag at home plate. The drill continues in the same manner until all outfielders have thrown one ball each to the catcher. The catchers then rotate.

By using all of the outfielders in these different positions, the throws to home plate will vary giving the catcher all types of throws to handle.

NOTE: FULL PROTECTIVE CATCHING GEAR SHOULD BE WORN BY THE CATCHER WHEN IN THE DEFENSIVE POSITION. IT IS UNDERSTOOD THAT DURING THE GAME THERE ARE TIMES THAT THE FACE MASK WILL BE REMOVED AND THROWN OUT OF THE LINE OF PLAY.

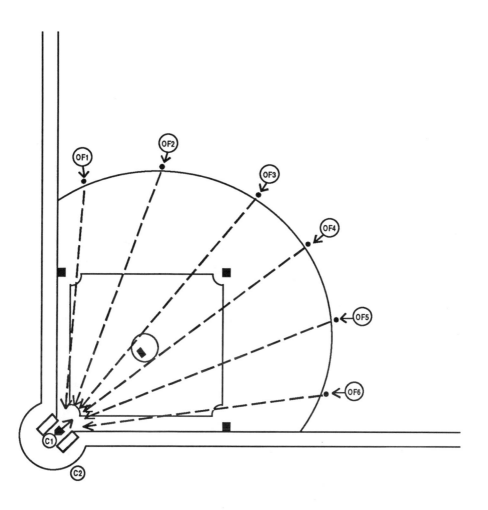

Tag Play Drill

Catcher's and Cut-Off Person's Communication Drill

Objective:

To improve communications between the catcher and the cut-off person on throws from the outfield.

Set-Up:

The catcher, first baseman, second baseman, third baseman, and shortstop are at their defensive positions.

Three to six outfielders are 10-20 feet behind the edge of the outfield grass. The outfielders have 3 balls each.

Directions:

When ready, the first baseman moves to the cut-off position and lines up with outfielder 1 for a throw to home plate. As the ball is coming to home, the catcher communicates with the cut-off person as to "cut the ball and take it back to a specific base" or "let it go". For example, "cut 2" means cut the ball and throw back to second base. The drill continues in the same manner until the outfielders have throw one ball each to home plate.

When the ball is coming in from the left side of the outfield, the shortstop moves into position to be the relay person if needed, and the second baseman covers second base. When the ball is coming in from the right side of the outfield, the second baseman moves into position to be the relay person if needed, and the shortstop covers second base.

NOTE: FULL PROTECTIVE CATCHING GEAR SHOULD BE WORN BY THE CATCHER WHEN IN THE DEFENSIVE POSITION. IT IS UNDERSTOOD THAT DURING THE DRILL THERE ARE TIMES THAT THE FACE MASK WILL BE REMOVED AND THROWN OUT OF THE LINE OF PLAY.

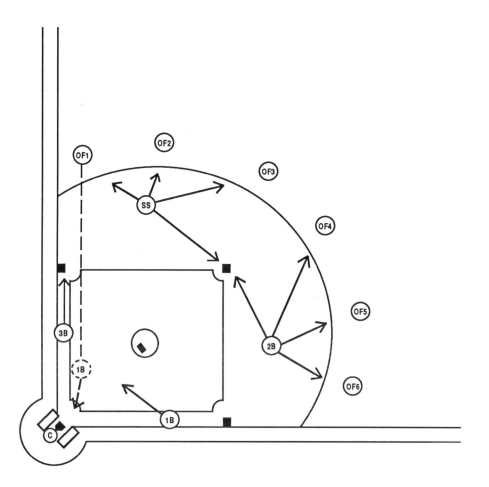

Catcher's and Cut-Off Person's
Communication Drill

From using the drills contained in this chapter, your catcher should improve on the following:

1. Strengthening the arms and shoulders for overhand throwing
2. Rolling the glove, so the glove is in the best position for reacting to the ball
3. Framing pitches and shifting on pitches that are slightly outside the width of the shoulders
4. Catching the outside of the ball on inside and outside corner pitches
5. Blocking balls pitched into the dirt
6. Blocking wild pitches thrown to the left, right, and in front of home plate
7. Fielding bunts and throwing to specific bases
8. Communicating with other infielders on foul ball and pop fly locations
9. Catching foul balls
10. Quickly taking the ball out of the glove
11. Quickly releasing the ball on throws
12. Throwing out runners on steal attempts
13. Catching throws from the outfield and making tag plays at home plate
14. Catching throws from the infield and making throws to first base
15. Communicating with the cut-off person on throws from the outfield

Hitting Drills

Drills for improving the following hitting skills are presented in this chapter:
1. Assuming the correct batting stance
2. Opening of the hips
3. Performing the proper stride
4. Using the correct hitting technique
5. Increasing bat velocity
6. Extending the lead arm
7. Extending the back arm
8. Increasing eye contact with the ball
9. Increasing hitting accuracy
10. Increasing the hitter's concentration during specific game situations

Also, there are drills for strengthening the muscles utilized in hitting.

The drills in this chapter are divided into five sections. The sections range from station drills to game situation drills. Each section is explained in detail. Depending on the skill level and needs of your players, you can start with any section. However, it is recommended that you stay with that section until your players demonstrate an understanding of the drills before beginning another drill section. Once two or more sections have been completed, you can select drills from each of the completed sections to form a batting practice. Also, it is necessary for your players to have an understanding of the hitting drills in sections 1 and 2 before they can practice the hitting drills in section 4.

In order to accomplish the hitting drill objectives in the most efficient manner, it is recommended that you organize the drills in sections 1, 2, and 3 in one of the following drill arrangements:

1. Circuit
2. Partners
3. Mass

For example, if the drills of section 1 were organized in a circuit arrangement, you would have six stations with three to four players assigned to each station. The players would work at their station for a designated time period or for a set number of repetitions and then rotate clockwise to the next station.

Batting Stance	Hip Turn	Stride	Lead Arm	Back Arm	Eye Contact
OOO --->	OOO --->	OOO --->	OOO --->	OOO --->	OOO ---

Circuit Arrangement

If the drills of Section 1 were organized into a partner arrangement, you would divide the players into partners. The partners would work together for a designated time period or for a set number of repetitions on a specific drill selected by the coach.

O	O	O	O	O	O
O	O	O	O	O	O

Partner Arrangement

If the drills of section 1 were organized into a mass arrangement, the players would all work on the same drill at the same time for a designated time period or for a set number of repetitions. The coach would select the specific drill to be practiced.

Mass Arrangement

Hitting Drills

Section 1

Station
Hitting Drills

1. Batting stance drill
2. Hip turn drill
3. Stride drill
4. Lead arm extension drill
5. Back arm extension drill
6. Eye contact drill

Section 2

Individual
Hitting Drills

1. Soft toss drill
2. One-knee hitting drill
3. Tee drill
4. Short throw drill
5. Quick hit drill
6. Pepper drill

Section 3

Hitting
Strength Drills

1. Wrist snap drill
2. Wrist roller drill
3. Partner resistance drill
4. Resistance swing drill

Section 4

Team
Hitting Drills

1. Batting practice drill #1
2. Batting practice drill #2
3. Batting practice drill #3
4. Batting practice drill #4

Section 5

Game Situation
Hitting Drills

1. Three-two count game
2. Two pitch game
3. Hit and run game
4. Nine outs game

Section 1:
Station Hitting Drills

Batting Stance Drill

Objective:

To improve the hitter's batting stance.

Directions:

The hitter assumes the regular batting stance with the coach checking the placement of the feet, knees, hips, shoulders, head, and eyes.

Hip Turn Drill

Objective:

To improve the opening of the hips during hitting.

Directions:

The hitter places the bat behind the back and interlocks both elbows. Without moving the feet, the hitter whips the hips open. The coach should make sure that the hitter pivots on the ball of the rear foot.

Stride Drill

Objective:

To practice the proper stride for hitting.

Directions:

The hitter assumes the regular batting stance and isolates the stride by taking a low, quick and soft stride forward. The coach should make sure the hitter is not moving the weight too far forward during the stride because this causes the hips to be thrown forward.

A   B

Hip Turn Drill

A   B

Stride Drill

Lead Arm Extension Drill

Objective:

To improve lead arm extension for hitting.

Directions:

The hitter assumes the regular batting stance with the front hand on the bat and the back hand placed behind the back. The hitter takes a form swing, and the coach checks for the lead arm extension.

Coaching Hint:

Some hitters might have to choke up on the bat or use a lighter bat to perform this drill.

Back Arm Extension Drill

Objective:

To improve back arm extension for hitting.

Directions:

The hitter assumes the regular batting stance with the back hand on the bat and the front hand placed behind the back. The hitter takes a form swing, and the coach checks for back arm extension.

Coaching Hint:

Some hitters might have to choke up on the bat or use a lighter bat to perform this drill.

Eye Contact Drill

Objective:

To improve eye contact with the ball.

Directions:

There are three players to a group (hitter, thrower, and catcher). The hitter stands 30-40 feet away from the thrower, and the catcher is in a catching position behind the hitter. The thrower throws the ball to the catcher, and the hitter watches the ball in from the release of the pitch to the hitter's contact point. The catcher does not need to wear catching gear because the hitter does not swing at the ball.

Coaching Hint:

Depending on your coaching philosophy, you could allow the hitter to watch the ball from the release of the pitch to the catcher.

A   **B**

Lead Arm Extension Drill

A   **B**

Back Arm Extension Drill

Section 2:
Individual Hitting Drills

Soft Toss Drill

Objective:

To increase the number of practice swings a hitter can perform using the correct technique.

Directions:

The hitter stands 12-15 feet away from a screen or fence. The tosser kneels on one knee 12 feet in front and to the side of the hitter and tosses the ball softly underhanded into the hitter's strike zone, so the hitter can take a full swing.

One-Knee Hitting Drill

Objectives:

1. To improve bat velocity.
2. To increase the number of practice swings a hitter can perform using the correct technique.

Directions:

The hitter kneels 12-15 feet away from a screen or fence. The hitter's right knee is on a towel and the left knee is bent at approximately a 90-degree angle. The tosser kneels on one knee 12 feet in front and to the side of the hitter and tosses balls underhanded into the hitter's strike zone, so the hitter can take a full swing.

Quick Hit Drill

Objectives:

1. To increase the strength and quickness of the hands for hitting.
2. To increase the number of practice swings a hitter can perform using the correct technique.

Directions:

The hitter stands 12-15 feet away from a screen or fence. The tosser kneels on one knee 12 feet in front and to the side of the hitter and tosses the ball underhanded at a fast rate into the hitter's strike zone, so the hitter can take a full swing. The hitter swings hard at the ball, and after each swing, the bat is rapidly returned to the ready position.

Soft Toss Drill

One-Knee Hitting Drill

Tee Drill

Objective:

To increase the number of practice swings a hitter can perform using the correct technique.

Directions:

For this drill, you need to buy or construct batting tees. Position the batting tees at different heights and let the hitter assume a stance in relation to the tee. This drill allows the hitter to hit pitches that are inside, outside, high, low, and down the middle.

Short Throw Drill

Objectives:

1. To eliminate overstriding while hitting.
2. To increase the number of practice swings a hitter can perform using the correct technique.

Directions:

This drill can be performed in a batting cage or against a backstop. (NOTE: A PROTECTIVE SCREEN IS NEEDED FOR YOUR THROWER'S SAFETY). The hitter takes a position 15 feet in front of a teammate or coach, who is seated behind the protective screen. The coach or teammate throws the ball from behind the protective screen with an overhand motion into the strike zone.

NOTE: Since this drill is designed to eliminate overstriding while hitting, it is not significant that the ball is thrown to the hitter with an overhand motion.

Pepper Drill

Objectives:

1. To improve controlled hitting.
2. To practice fielding ground balls.

Directions:

From three to six players are in a line in the defensive position. The hitter stands 20 feet in front and away from the players. One of the players throws a ball to the hitter, and the hitter concentrates on swinging down on the ball and hitting the ball back to the players.

Tee Drill

Short Throw Drill

Section 3:
Hitting Strength Drills

Wrist Snap Drill

Objective:

To increase wrist and hand strength for hitting.

Directions:

The hitter assumes a hitting stance and places the bat into the hitting zone. The hitter breaks the wrists back and forth for a designated time period or until fatigued.

Wrist Roller Drill

Objective:

To increase wrist and hand strength for hitting.

Directions:

Have a 3-foot rope attached to an 18-inch wooden rod and have an appropriate size weight for the strength of your athletes secured to the end of the rope. The hitter holds the wooden rod in front of the body and rolls the rod forward until the entire rope is rolled onto the wooden rod. Then reverse the procedure, and unwind the rope by rolling the hands and wrists backwards.

Partner Resistance Drill

Objective:

To increase wrist and hand strength for hitting.

Directions:

Partners face each other, and both partners place hands about shoulder width apart on a bat held in front of them. Both partners try to rotate the bat backwards without pulling the bat toward themselves.

Resistance Swing Drill

Objective:

To increase the strength of the muscles utilized in hitting.

Directions:

The hitter assumes a hitting stance with a partner standing directly behind the hitter. The partner places one hand about 3-4 inches from the end of the bat. The hitter takes a normal swing with the bat, using correct form, while the partner applies resistance to the bat. While the hitter swings, the partner continues to apply a resistance to the bat and walks around the hitter in order to allow the hitter to go through the entire range of motion for the swing.

Section 4:
Team Hitting Drills

Batting Practice Drill #1

Objectives:

1. To provide an equal amount of hitting time for all players.
2. To provide practice for the defensive team in a game-like situation.

Set-Up:

Divide the team into two squads. One squad is the defensive team, and the other squad is divided into four stations.

Station 1 has a hitter and an on-deck hitter.

Station 2 has two players working at batting tees.

Station 3 has two players performing station hitting drills.

Station 4 has two players working on bunting.

Directions:

Players work at each station for 7 minutes.

Station 1: The hitter takes ten hits with the pitcher pitching the ball and then rotates with the on-deck hitter, who has been taking practice swings in the on-deck circle. The defensive squad works on game situations. Periodically, the catcher or head coach calls out a game situation, such as "bases loaded with one out."

Station 2: The hitters hit into protective screens or a fence. The hitters vary their stances in relation to the batting tees, so they can hit inside, outside, and down the middle pitches.

Station 3: The two hitters perform five station drills in a circuit arrangement. The hitters perform five or more repetitions at each station and then repeat the sequence.

Station 4: One player hits eight repetitions of each type of bunt, while the other player serves as the tosser.

After 28 minutes, the two squads rotate positions.

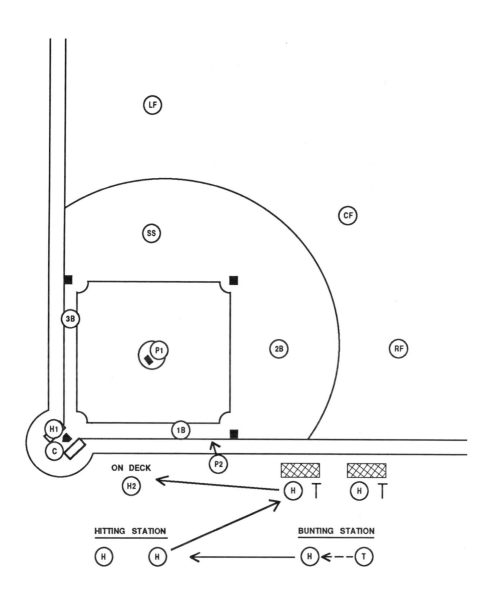

Batting Practice Drill #1

Batting Practice Drill #2

Objectives:

1. To provide an equal amount of hitting time for all players.
2. To provide practice for the defensive team in a game-like situation.

Set-Up:

The drill has three stations.
Station 1 consists of the defensive players.
Station 2 consists of the hitters.
Station 3 consists of the baserunners.

Directions:

Divide the team into two infield and outfield groups. For example, the groups can be composed of the following players:

Group 1 — first baseman, second baseman, third baseman, and shortstop.
Group 2 — catcher, left fielder, center fielder, and right fielder.
Group 3 — first baseman. second baseman, third baseman, and shortstop.
Group 4 — catcher, left fielder, center fielder, and right fielder.

The groups rotate in the following manner every 20 minutes:

Time	Defensive Players	Hitters	Baserunners
	(Groups)	(Group)	(Group)
First 20 minutes	1 & 2	3	4
Second 20 minutes	1 & 4	2	3
Third 20 minutes	3 & 4	1	2
Fourth 20 minutes	2 & 3	4	1

All four groups practice in a game-like situation.

The coach can put baserunners on different bases to set up a particular defensive situation.

The pitchers rotate every 20 minutes in order to pitch to different groups.

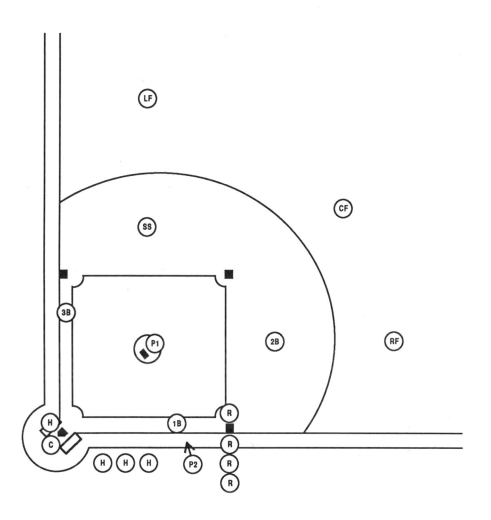

Batting Practice Drill #2

Batting Practice Drill #3

Objectives:

1. To provide an equal amount of hitting time for all players.
2. To provide practice for the defensive team in a game-like situation.

Set-Up:

The team is divided into two groups. Group 1 consists of the hitters and baserunners, and group 2 consists of the defensive players, who are at the defensive positions.

Baserunners are at first, second, and third bases.

Hitter 1 is in the batter's box, while hitter 2 is on the right side of home plate, hitter 3 is on the left side of home plate, hitter 4 is off the field in the vicinity of third base, and hitter 5 is off the field in the vicinity of first base.

The head coach is in the third base coaching box, and the assistant coach is in the first base coaching box.

A protective screen is on the left side of hitter 2, and a protective screen is on the right side of hitter 3. A protective screen can be placed in front of the first baseman's defensive position, but it is optional.

Directions:

Hitter 1 hits for 4 minutes. During that time when there is no defensive or offensive action going on, hitter 2 acts as a fungo hitter and hits ground balls to the third baseman and shortstop. During that same time, hitter 3 acts as a fungo hitter and hits ground balls to the second baseman. Hitters 2 and 3 have to alternate hitting to their specific areas. Whenever a ball is fielded from a fungo hitter, the ball is thrown back to that particular fungo hitter. Hitters 4 and 5 hit off batting tees and into protective screens or a fence. The hitters vary their stances in relation to the hitting tees, so they can hit inside, outside, and down the middle pitches.

The baserunners are running the bases similar to a game-like situation. However, the defensive unit may assume that only certain bases are occupied, depending on the situation they choose to work on. All baserunners move up a base after each defensive play.

After 4 minutes of the drill, group 1 rotates in the following manner: hitter 5 moves to hitter 4's location, hitter 4 moves to hitter 3's location, hitter 3 moves to hitter 2's location, hitter 2 moves to hitter 1's location, hitter 1 becomes a baserunner, and one of the baserunners moves to hitter 5's location.

After group 1 completes the circuit, they rotate with group 2, and the drill is repeated.

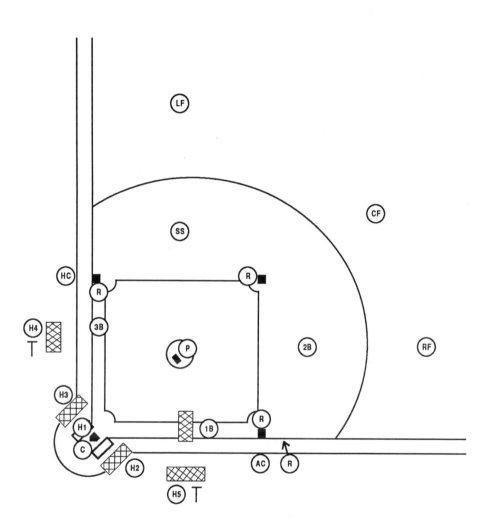

Batting Practice Drill #3

Batting Practice Drill #4 (Part A)

Objectives:

1. To provide an equal amount of hitting time for all players.
2. To provide practice for the defensive team in a game-like situation.

Set-Up:

The team is divided into two squads. Squad 1 consists of the infielders, and squad 2 consists of the outfielders.

Squad 1 starts with the infielders at their defensive positions, along with one player serving as hitter 1 and another player serving as the on-deck hitter.

A full ball bucket is at the pitching area, and an empty ball bucket is at each base.

Squad 2 starts at three hitting stations, which consist of two players each. Station 1 is at the batting cage. Station 2 is at the batting tees and has two batting tees and two protective screens. Station 3 is in the bunting area and has a full ball bucket.

Directions:

Squad 1: Hitter 1 hits for 4½ minutes off a pitcher. The first five pitches thrown to hitter 1 are bunted, and the rest of the pitches are hit away. At the same time, the on-deck hitter takes practice swings.

After 4½ minutes, hitter 1 rotates to a defensive position, the on-deck hitter becomes hitter 1, and an infielder becomes the on-deck hitter.

The infielders play out different situations such as: for the first hitter, the infielders throw to first base; for the second hitter, the infielders turn a double play; for the third hitter, the infielders throw to third base; for the fourth hitter, the infielders throw home; for the fifth hitter, the infielders check the runner at third base and throw to first base; and for the sixth hitter, the infielders throw home and the catcher throws back to first base for the second out.

Squad 2: (Station 1) One player hits off the pitching machine working on specific game situations, while the other player serves as the feeder. The hitter rotates with the feeder after each bucket of balls has been hit.

(Station 2) The two hitters hit off the batting tees. The hitters vary their stances in relation to the batting tees, so they can hit inside, outside, and down the middle pitches.

(Station 3) One player hits eight repetitions of each type of bunt, while the other player serves as the tosser. After completing this sequence, the players rotate.

After 9 minutes, the hitters rotate stations in the following manner: station 1 moves to station 2, station 2 moves to station 3, and station 3 moves to station 1.

After 30 minutes, squads 1 and 2 rotate practice areas and begin Batting Practice Drill #4 (Part B).

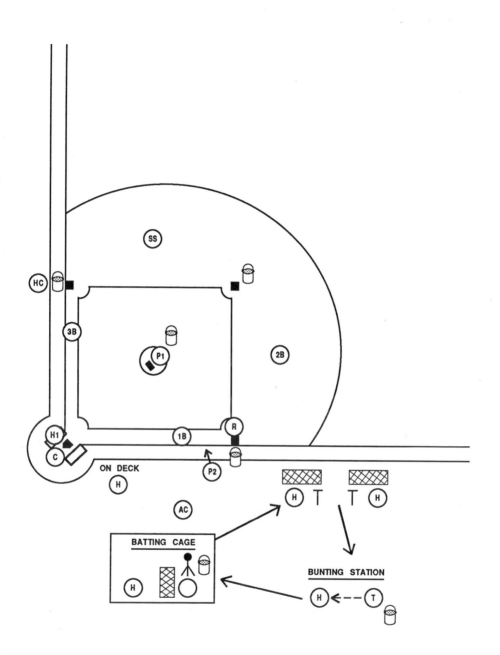

Batting Practice Drill #4 (Part A)

Batting Practice Drill #4 (Part B)

Objectives:

1. To provide an equal amount of hitting time for all players.
2. To provide practice for the defensive team in a game-like situation.

Set-Up:

Squad 1 starts at the three hitting stations, which consist of two players each.

Squad 2 starts with three outfielders at their defensive positions, one player behind second base and protected by a screen, one player serving as hitter 1, and one player on the right side of the hitter and serving as the on-deck hitter.

The head coach is in the vicinity of third base.

Both the on-deck hitter and the head coach have a full ball bucket. Also a full ball bucket is at the pitching area, and an empty ball bucket is behind second base.

Directions:

Squad 1: The directions are the same as for Squad 2 of Batting Practice Drill #4 (Part A).

Squad 2: Hitter 1 hits for 4½ minutes off a pitcher. The first five pitches thrown to hitter 1 are bunted, and the rest of the pitches are hit away. During that time, when there is no offensive action going on, the on-deck hitter acts as a fungo hitter and hits balls to the right fielder and center fielder. During that same time, the head coach acts as a fungo hitter and hits balls to the left fielder and center fielder. The on-deck hitter and the head coach alternate hitting to their specific areas. Balls fielded from hitter 1 are thrown to the player behind second base, while balls fielded from the fungo hitters are thrown back to that particular fungo hitter.

After 4½ minutes, hitter 1 rotates to an outfielder's defensive position, a defensive player moves behind second base, the player behind second base becomes the on-deck hitter, and the on-deck hitter becomes hitter 1.

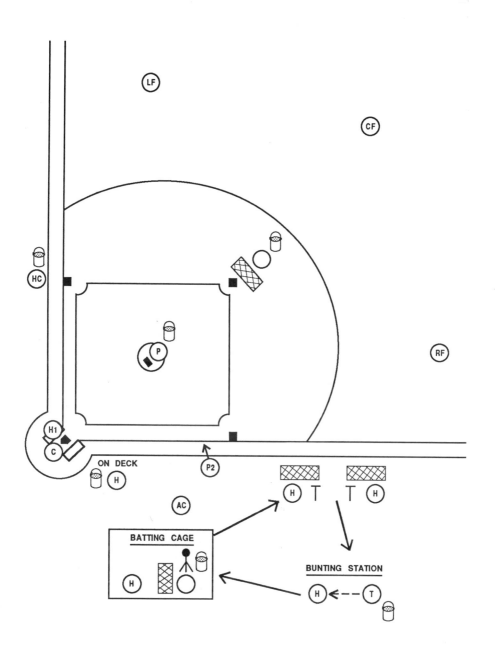

Batting Practice Drill #4 (Part B)

Section 5:

Hitting Drills for Game Situations

Objectives for Hitting Drills in Section 5:

1. To practice on specific game situations.
2. To improve the player's concentration during specific game situations.

Set-Up for Hitting Drills in Section 5:

The team is divided into two squads for playing intrasquad games.

Directions:

1. Three-Two Count Game

The teams play an intrasquad game with each batter going to the plate with a 3-2 count. The defensive and offensive teams play the 3-2 game with the same rules that thay would play a regulation game.

Variation: Runners are placed on the different bases to start each inning.

2. Two Pitch Game

The teams play an intrasquad game with each batter going to the plate getting only two pitches. If the batter hits the first pitch, the batter runs the bases in a game-like manner. If the batter takes the first pitch, the batter has one more pitch to hit or it counts as an out. The defensive and the offensive teams play the two pitch game with the same rules that they would play a regulation game.

Variation: Runners are placed on the different bases to start each inning.

3. Hit and Run Game

Runners are placed on the different bases prior to each inning. The teams play an intrasquad game with each batter going to the plate in a hit and run situation. The defensive and the offensive teams play the hit and run game with the same rules that they would play a regulation game.

4. Nine Outs Game

The teams play an intrasquad game with the defensive team staying on the field for nine outs, instead of three. The bases are cleared, and a new inning is started after three outs.

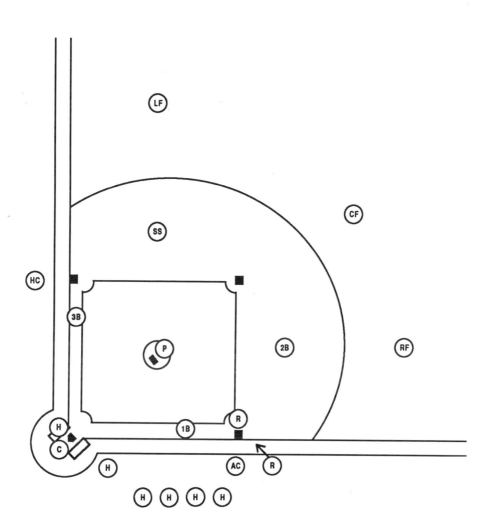

Hitting Drills for Game Situations

From using the drills contained in this chapter, your athletes should improve on the following:

1. Assuming the correct batting stance
2. Opening of the hips during hitting
3. Performing the proper stride for hitting
4. Using the correct hitting technique
5. Increasing bat velocity
6. Extending the lead arm
7. Extending the back arm
8. Increasing eye contact with the ball
9. Strengthening the muscles utilized in hitting
10. Increasing hitting accuracy
11. Increasing concentration during specific game situations

Bunting Drills

Drills for improving the following bunting skills are presented in this chapter:
1. Executing the different types of bunts
   a. Sacrifice
   b. Drag
   c. Slap
   d. Squeeze
2. Increasing bunting accuracy
3. Executing the squeeze play
4. Executing the bunt and run play

Basic Bunting Drill

Objective:

To learn the different types of bunts.

Set-Up:

Drill has one hitter and one tosser. The tosser is 25 feet from the hitter and kneels on one knee.

Drill can have as many groups as desired.

Directions:

The tosser throws the hitter ten balls, while the hitter practices on one type of bunt. After the hitter hits ten bunts, the hitter and tosser rotate. The drill may be repeated as many times as desired practicing the different types of bunts.

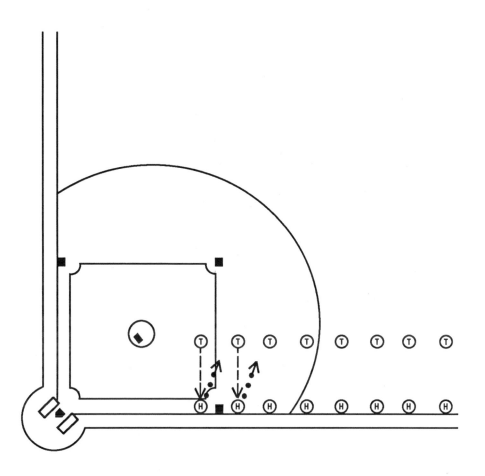

Basic Bunting Drill

Bunting Accuracy Drill

Objective:

To improve the player's accuracy in bunting to a specific area.

Set-Up:

A rope is placed 15 feet from home plate and in a semicircle stretching from one sideline to another.

The pitcher and catcher are at their defensive positions. The pitcher has a full ball bucket, and the catcher has an empty ball bucket.

All hitters are at home plate.

Directions:

Each hitter bunts the ball and tries to keep it inside the rope. The hitter gets two chances to contact the bunt. If the first or second ball is bunted, the hitter runs to first base. If the hitter misses both balls, the hitter runs all the bases before returning to the end of the line.

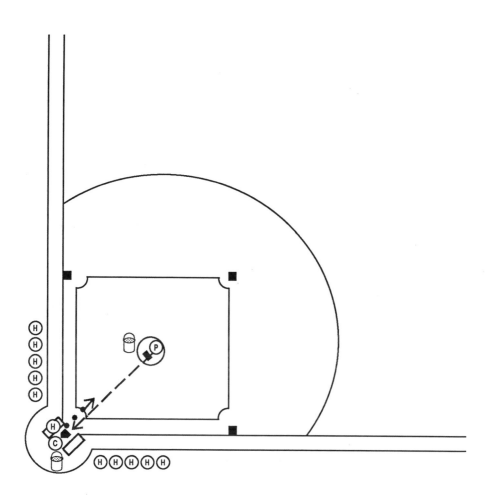

Bunting Accuracy Drill

Bunting Technique Drill

Objective:

To improve the player's bunting technique.

Set-Up:

A protective screen is in the middle of the pitching area.

Drill has two pitchers and two catchers. Pitcher 1 is in front of the protective screen and throws to home plate. Pitcher 2 is behind the protective screen and throws to second base.

Each pitcher has a full ball bucket, and each catcher has an empty ball bucket.

The hitters are divided into two groups, with one group at home plate and the other group at second base.

Directions:

Hitter 1 bunts a specific bunt and runs to first base, while at the same time, hitter 2 bunts a specific bunt and runs to third base. Then both hitters jog to the ends of the opposite lines.

For time efficiency, the balls not contacted by the hitter are placed in the catcher's ball bucket, thereby allowing the pitcher to prepare for the next pitch.

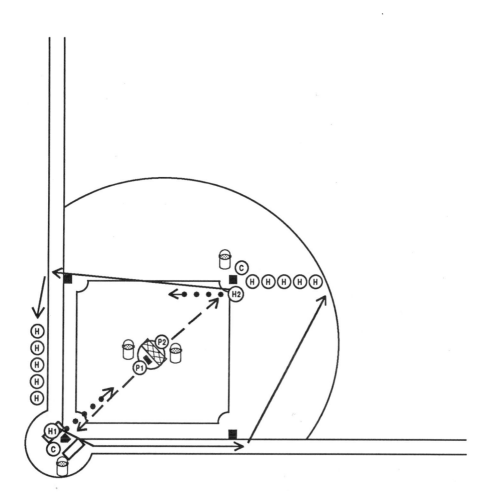

Bunting Technique Drill

Bunting Series Drill

Objectives:

1. To improve the player's ability to execute the different types of bunts.
2. To improve the baserunner's ability to react to different bunt situations.

Set-Up for All Rounds:

The pitcher, catcher, first baseman, second baseman, third baseman, and shortstop are at their defensive positions.

Half of the players are at home plate as hitters, while the other half of the players serve as baserunners. The locations of the baserunners vary with the rounds and are stated in the directions for the rounds.

Directions:

For All of the Rounds: After the hitter runs through first base, the hitter goes to the end of the runner's line. After the runner reaches the designated base, the runner jogs to the end of the hitter's line.

Round 1:

1. The hitter bunts a sacrifice bunt and runs to first base. After taking an aggressive lead, the runner at first base looks to see if the bunt has been put down, and runs to second base.
2. The hitter bunts a sacrifice bunt and runs to first base. After taking an aggressive lead, the runner at second base looks to see if the bunt has been put down, and runs to third base. It is recommended that the hitter put the bunt down in the vicinity of third base or the pitching area.
3. The hitter bunts a sacrifice bunt and runs to first base. After taking an aggressive lead, the runners at first and second bases look to see if the bunt has been put down, and run to second and third bases, respectively. It is recommended that the hitter put the bunt down in the vicinity of third base or the pitching area.

Round 2:

1. The hitter bunts a drag bunt and runs to first base. After taking an aggressive lead, the runner at first base looks to see if the bunt has been put down, and runs to second base.
2. The hitter bunts a drag bunt and runs to first base. After taking an aggressive lead, the runner at second base looks to see if the bunt has been put down, and runs to third base.

Bunting Series Drill
(Continued)

3. The hitter bunts a drag bunt and runs to first base. After taking an aggressive lead, the runners at first and second bases look to see if the bunt has been put down, and run to second and third bases, respectively.

4. The hitter bunts a drag bunt and runs to first base. After taking an aggressive lead, the runner at third base waits for the release of the throw to first base, and then breaks for home.

Round 3:

1. The hitter, who is in a squeeze play situation, bunts the ball and runs to first base. The runner at first base breaks with the pitch and without hesitating, runs to third base. It is recommended that the hitter put the bunt down in the vicinity of third base or the pitching area.

2. The hitter, who is in a squeeze play situation, bunts the ball and runs to first base. The runner at third base breaks with the pitch and without hesitating, runs home. It is recommended that the hitter put the bunt down in the vicinity of third base or the pitching area.

Round 4:

1. The hitter bunts a slap bunt and runs to first base. After taking an aggressive lead, the runner at first base looks to see if the bunt has been executed, and runs to second base. It is recommended that the bunt be pushed in the direction of the second baseman or the shortstop.

2. The hitter bunts a slap bunt and runs to first base. After taking an aggressive lead, the runner at second base looks to see if the bunt has been executed, and runs to third base. It is recommended that the bunt be pushed in the direction of the second baseman.

3. The hitter bunts a slap bunt to the second baseman and runs to first base. As soon as the runner at third base determines that the ball is going to the second baseman, the runner breaks for home.

Round 5:

1. The hitter, who is in a bunt and run situation, bunts the ball and runs to first base. The runner at first base leaves with the pitch and runs to second base.

2. The hitter, who is in a bunt and run situation, bunts the ball and runs to first base. The runner at second base leaves with the pitch and runs to third base.

Note: Generally, when running the bases aggressively, the baserunners slide into the bases on bunt situations.

From using the drills contained in this chapter, your athletes should improve on the following:

1. Executing the sacrifice, drag, slap, and squeeze bunts
2. Increasing bunting accuracy
3. Executing the squeeze play
4. Executing the bunt and run play
5. Quickly reacting to different bunt situations when serving as a baserunner

9

Baserunning Drills

Drills for improving the following baserunning skills are presented in this chapter:
1. Baserunning mechanics
2. Increasing running speed
3. Increasing explosive power off a base
4. Increasing endurance for baserunning
5. Increasing the aggressiveness of the baserunner

Box Running Drill

Objective:

To improve the height of the runner's knee lift which is needed for proper baserunning mechanics.

Set-Up:

Drill is performed in the outfield.
Seven boxes are arranged in a row and spaced 3 feet apart.
The players are in a line facing the row of boxes.

Directions:

Each player runs the row of boxes using correct running technique. After the last player has finished running the boxes, the players reverse directions and run the boxes again. The drill continues for as long as desired.

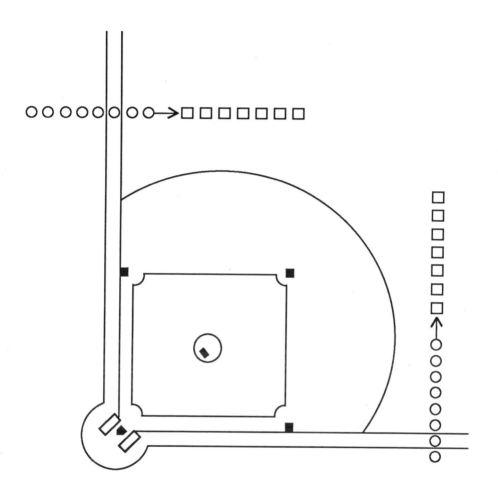

Box Running Drill

3-3-2-1 Running Drill

Objectives:

    1. To improve the mechanics of baserunning.
    2. To improve the player's overall conditioning.

Set-Up:

Drill can have as many runners as desired in a line at home plate.

The head coach is in the third base coaching box, and the assistant coach is in the first base coaching box.

Directions:

The runner sprints to first base and jogs back to home plate, repeating three times.

The runner sprints to second base and continues to round the bases by jogging to home plate, repeating three times.

The runner sprints to third base and jogs to home plate, repeating again.

Then the runner sprints a home run.

Coaching Hint:

It would be beneficial for your players to perform the drill in a game-like situation and to make eye contact with the baserunning coaches.

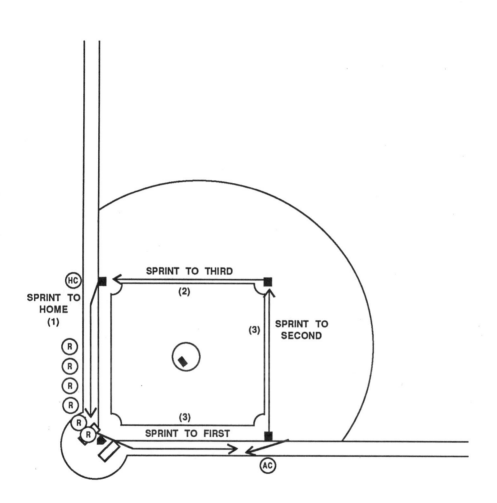

3-3-2-1 Running Drill

Indian Relay Drill

Objective:

To improve the player's speed.

Set-Up:

The team is divided into two groups of eight players each. Each group is in a line with one player behind the other.

The drill is conducted within the boundaries of the ball field.

Directions:

The first line of players starts to jog with equal distance between the players. (It is important for the players to maintain equal distance between themselves for the drill to proceed properly.) Upon a signal given by the first person in line, the last player in line moves out of formation to the right and sprints to the front of the line. The runner then slows to a jog, and upon another signal, the last person in line sprints to the front of the line. This sequence continues for as long as desired.

When there is adequate room, the second line of players starts to jog.

Variation:

The first person in line has a ball. As the group jogs, the first player in line tosses the ball overhead to the next person, and the sequence continues until the last person in line receives the ball. Upon receiving the ball, the last player in line sprints to the front of the line, and the drill continues for as long as desired.

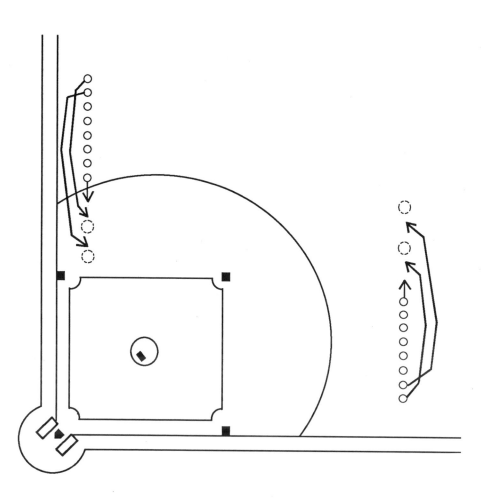

Indian Relay Drill

Explosive Power Drill

Objective:

To improve the player's explosive power off a base.

Set-Up:

Drill has four lines of runners, with one line at each base. The lines consist of four or more runners.

Directions:

The first runner in each line explodes off the base for three to four steps, then jogs to the next base and goes to the end of the line at that base. The drill continues in this manner for a designated time period.

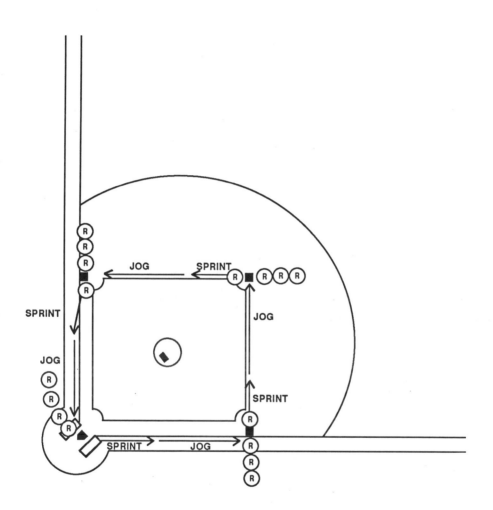

Explosive Power Drill

Resistance Running Drill

Objective:

To improve the player's explosive power off a base.

Set-Up:

Players 1 and 2 stand facing each other with player 1 standing on the right field sideline.

Directions:

Player 1 runs at full speed for 30 feet and drives player 2 back while player 2 applies a resistance to player 1's shoulders. The amount of resistance applied to player 1 should not prevent the player from using correct running form.

After player 1 has performed the drill five to ten times, the players rotate positions.

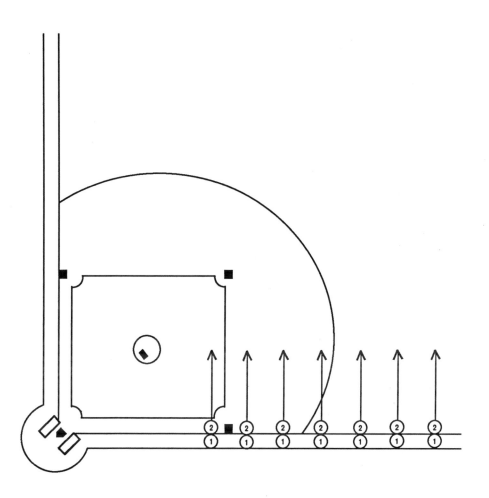

Resistance Running Drill

Sprint Baserunning Drill

Objectives:

    1. To improve the player's overall conditioning.
    2. To improve the player's explosive power and speed.

Set-Up:

Drill can have as many runners as desired in a line at home plate.

Directions:

The runner sprints to first base, jogs to the outfield fence along the right field sideline, and jogs back to first base (making a loop at first base in order to get in line with second base).

As soon as the runner touches first base, the runner sprints to second base, jogs to the center field fence, and jogs back to second base (again making a loop at second base in order to get in line with third base).

As soon as the runner touches second base, the runner sprints to third base, jogs to the outfield fence along the left field sideline, jogs back to third base, and sprints to home plate. The drill is repeated as many times as desired.

Coaching Hint:

The player should overrun the bases in order to run the full distance between the bases.

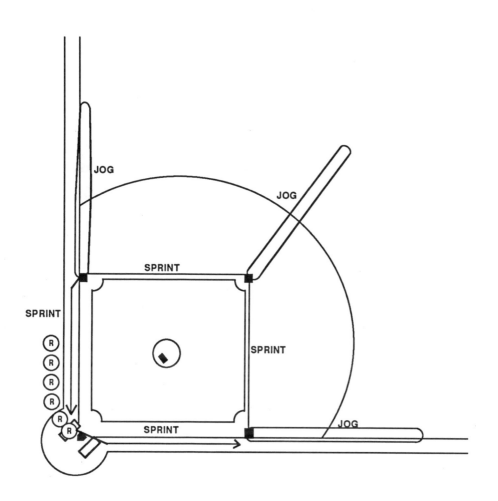

Sprint Baserunning Drill

Competition Running Drill

Objective:

To improve the player's speed in running a single.

Set-Up:

Drill can have as many runners as desired in lines at first base and third base.

The head coach is at home plate, and the assistant coach is at second base.

Directions:

On the head coach's signal, the runner at first base tries to reach second base before the runner at third base reaches home plate. The runners then jog to the ends of the opposite lines.

Variations:

1. The runner at home plate tries to reach second base before the runner at second base reaches home plate.

2. The runner at home plate tries to reach third base before the runner at first base reaches home plate.

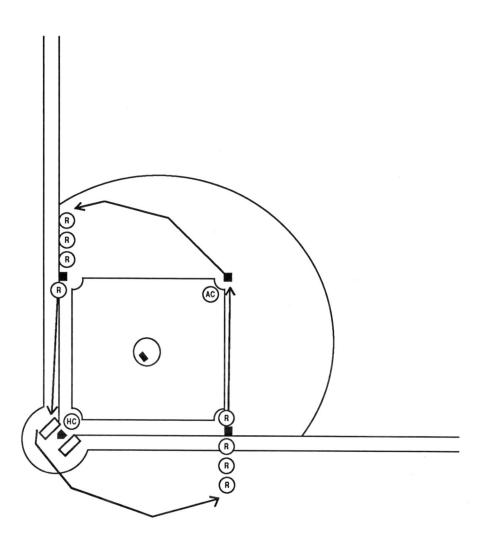

Competition Running Drill

Chase Running Drill

Objectives:

1. To improve the player's explosive power off a base.
2. To improve the player's speed.

Set-Up:

Runner 1 is at first base, while runner 2 is 10 feet from first base and in the direction of second base.

The head coach is at first base, and the assistant coach is at second base.

Directions:

On the head coach's signal, runner 1 tries to catch runner 2 before runner 2 reaches second base.

Variations:

Drill can be performed using doubles, triples, and home runs.

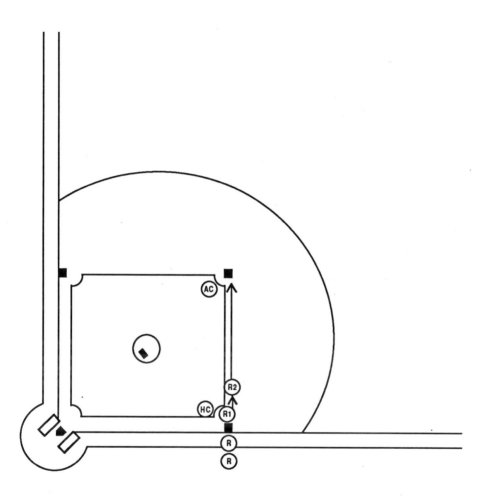

Chase Running Drill

Two Teams Running Drill

Objective:

To improve the player's endurance for baserunning.

Set-Up:

Drill has two teams of runners, with one team of runners in a line at home plate, and the other team of runners in a line at second base.

The head coach is in the pitching area.

Directions:

On the coach's signal, the first person in each line runs all the bases and then tags the next runner in line, who runs all the bases. Each team tries to catch the other team's runner.

The coach needs to make sure the runner touches every base and tags the next player in line.

Coaching Hint:

You can divide your team into two groups of equal speed. At the beginning of the drill, it may appear that the two runners will never catch each other. However, after a period of time, the drill usually becomes very exciting and motivating because one runner eventually overtakes the other runner, due to either less speed or poor baserunning mechanics.

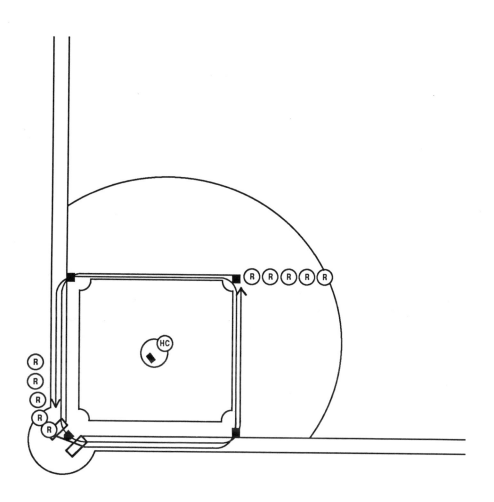

Two Teams Running Drill

Take Two Running Drill

Objective:

To improve the aggressiveness of the runner to advance toward another base.

Set-Up:

Drill has one hitter, who is near the pitching area, and one shagger, who is standing on the right side of the hitter.

The first baseman, second baseman, shortstop, center fielder, and left fielder are at their defensive positions.

Drill can have as many runners as desired in a line at home plate.

Directions:

The hitter hits a ground ball toward the center fielder or left fielder. At the same time, the runner runs to first base and rounds the base, while noticing if the outfielder has cleanly fielded the ball. If the ball has been fielded, the runner quickly returns to first base. If the ball is mishandled, the runner advances to second base. Once the outfielder has fielded the ball, the outfielder throws the ball to the shortstop, who is the cut-off person in line with second base.

Variation:

The hitter hits to the outfielders making them move to field the ball.

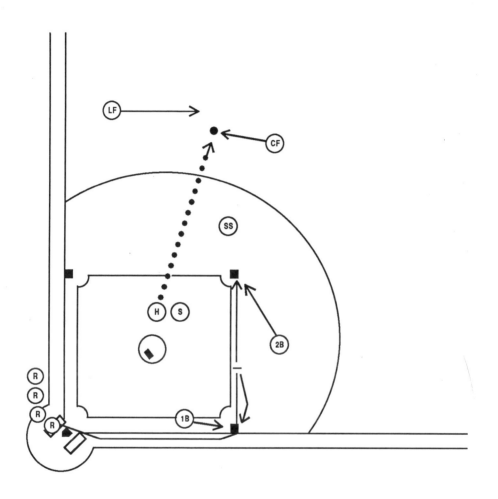

Take Two Running Drill

From using the drills contained in this chapter, your athletes should improve on the following:

1. Baserunning mechanics
2. Increasing running speed
3. Increasing explosive power off a base
4. Increasing endurance for baserunning
5. Increasing the aggressiveness to advance to another base

10

Sliding Drills

Drills for improving the following sliding techniques are presented in this chapter:
1. Determining the "tucked leg" for sliding
2. Executing the different types of slides
   A. Bent-leg
   B. Pop-up
   C. Hook
   D. Head-first

Mass Sliding Drill

Objective:

To determine the player's "tucked leg" for sliding.

Set-Up:

All players are in the outfield in a mass drill formation. The head coach stands facing the group.

Directions:

The player sits on the ground with the arms extended in back to support the upper body. The legs are extended in front with the knees slightly bent. The player raises the body on the hands and feet and then falls backwards, while tucking one leg underneath in a "4" shape. When the player falls backwards, the arms are thrown in front of the body with the hands in the air.

A

B

Mass Sliding Drill

Basic Sliding Drill

Objective:

To learn different sliding techniques.

Set-Up:

The team is divided into two groups. Group 1 is in the outfield on the right sideline, and group 2 is in the outfield on the left sideline.

A 30-foot piece of cardboard is placed 30 feet away from each sideline. A moveable base is placed approximately 3 feet from the end of the cardboard.

The head coach and the assistant coach are at separate sliding stations in a position to help the players.

Directions:

The first player in each line runs toward the appropriate base and practices a particular sliding technique. After sliding, the players go to the ends of their respective lines, and the drill continues for as long as desired.

Pop-Up Sliding Drill

Objective:

To learn the pop-up sliding technique.

Set-Up:

All players are in the outfield in a mass drill formation.
The head coach stands facing the group.

Directions:

All players are on the ground in a bent leg sliding position. The players shift their weight forward onto the lead leg and stand up. The drill is repeated for as long as desired.

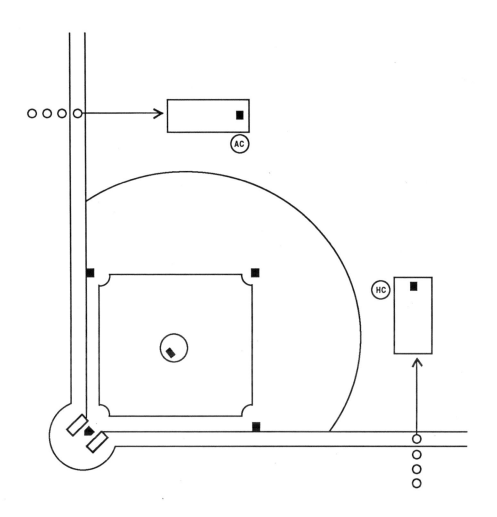

Basic Sliding Drill

Head-First Sliding Drill

Objective:

To improve the head-first sliding technique.

Set-Up:

All players are at home plate.

The manager is in left field on the edge of the outfield grass and has a full ball bucket. The head coach is near second base, and the assistant coach is in the coach's box at first base.

Directions:

The first runner runs to first base and is given a signal by the assistant coach to turn and look to see if it is possible to advance to second base. As the runner rounds first base, the runner locates the manager in left field. The manager is holding a ball. If the manager drops the ball, the runner advances to second base and performs a bent-leg slide. If the manager brings the ball back in a throwing motion and acts like the ball is going to be thrown to first base, the runner quickly returns to first base and performs a head-first slide.

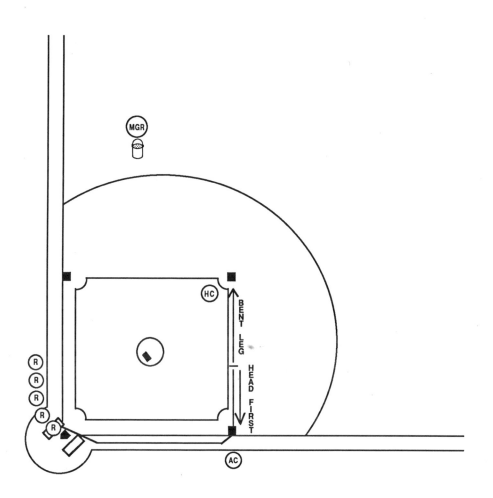

Head-First Sliding Drill

Multi-Sliding Drill

Objective:

To improve the different sliding techniques.

Set-Up:

Four or more runners are at each base.
The head coach is in the pitching area.

Directions:

The first runner in each line runs toward the next base and performs a specific slide. For example, the runner going into second base performs a bent-leg or pop-up slide, the runner going into third base performs a head-first slide, and the runner going into home performs a hook slide. After the runner slides at home plate, the runner jogs to first base, and the drill is repeated for as long as desired.

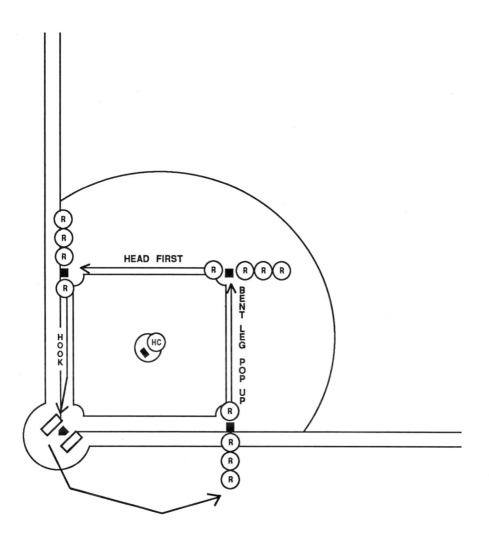

Multi-Sliding Drill

From using the drills contained in this chapter, your athletes should improve on the following:

1. Determining the "tucked leg" for sliding
2. Executing the bent-leg, pop-up, hook, and head-first slides

11

Bunt Defensive Drills

Drills for improving the following infielders' skills for bunt defense are presented in this chapter:
1. Executing the bunt defense with a runner at first base
2. Executing the bunt defense with a runner at second base
3. Executing the bunt defense with runners at first and second bases
4. Executing the bunt defense with a runner at third base
5. Executing the bunt defense for a squeeze play with a runner at first base
6. Executing the bunt defense for a squeeze play with a runner at third base

Bunt Defense with a Runner
at First Base Drill

Objective:

To improve the infielders' ability to execute the bunt defense with a runner at first base.

Set-Up for All Rounds:

The pitcher, catcher, first baseman, second baseman, third baseman, and shortstop are at their defensive positions.

Half of the players are at home plate as hitters, while the other half of the players serve as baserunners.

The head coach is in the third base coaching box, and the assistant coach is in the first base coaching box.

Directions:

Round 1:

The defense fields the bunt and throws the ball to first base. The second baseman, who has taken the throw at first base, checks the runner at second base to see if the runner has rounded the base.

Round 2:

The defense fields the bunt and throws the ball to first base. The second baseman, who has taken the throw at first base, throws the ball to second base to get out the runner, who has rounded the base.

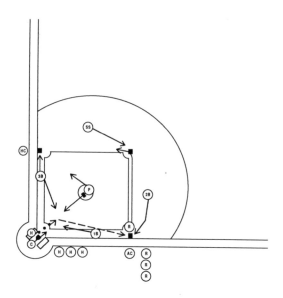

Round 1

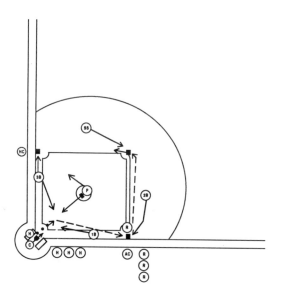

Round 2

Bunt Defense with a Runner
at First Base Drill

Bunt Defense with a Runner
at First Base Drill

(Continued)

Round 3:
The defense fields the bunt and throws the ball to second base with the shortstop turning the double play.

Round 4:
The defense fields the bunt and throws the ball to first base. The second baseman, who has taken the throw at first base, throws the ball to third base to get out the runner, who has tried to advance to third base on a squeeze play.

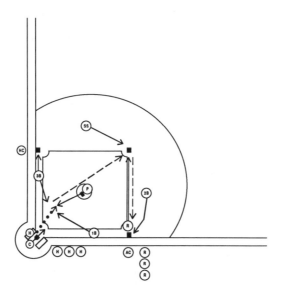

Round 3

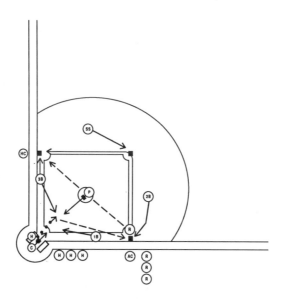

Round 4

Bunt Defense with a Runner
at First Base Drill

Bunt Defense with a Runner
at Second Base Drill

Objective:

To improve the infielders' ability to execute the bunt defense with a runner at second base.

Set-Up for All Rounds:

The pitcher, catcher, first baseman, second baseman, third baseman, and shortstop are at their defensive positions.

Half of the players are at home plate as hitters, while the other half of the players serve as baserunners.

The head coach is in the third base coaching box, and the assistant coach is in the first base coaching box.

Directions:

Round 1:

The defense fields the bunt and checks the runner advancing to third base. After realizing the defense cannot get the runner out at third base, the defense throws the ball to first base.

Round 2:

The defense fields the bunt and throws the ball to third base to get the runner out.

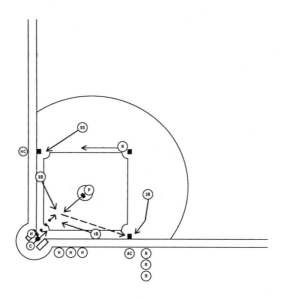

Round 1

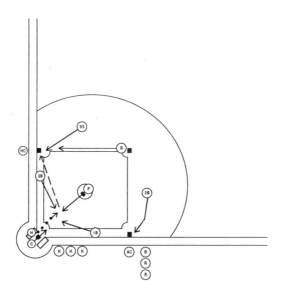

Round 2

Bunt Defense with a Runner
at Second Base Drill

Bunt Defense with Runners
at First and Second Bases Drill

Objective:

To improve the infielders' ability to execute the bunt defense with runners at first and second bases.

Set-Up for All Rounds:

The pitcher, catcher, first baseman, second baseman, third baseman, and shortstop are at their defensive positions.

Half of the players are at home plate as hitters, while the other half of the players serve as baserunners.

The head coach is in the third base coaching box, and the assistant coach is in the first base coaching box.

Directions:

Round 1:

The defense fields the bunt and checks the runner advancing to third base. After realizing the defense cannot get the runner out at third base, the defense throws the ball to first base.

Round 2:

The defense fields the bunt and throws the ball to second base with the second baseman turning the double play.

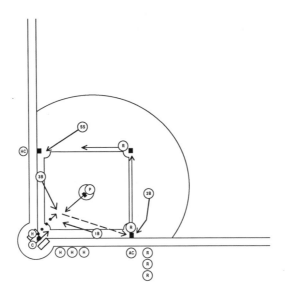

Round 1

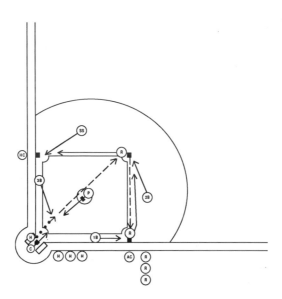

Round 2

Bunt Defense with Runners
at First and Second Bases Drill

Bunt Defense with Runners
at First and Second Bases Drill
(Continued)

Round 3:

The defense fields the bunt and throws the ball to third base with the shortstop covering the base. After getting the runner out, the shortstop checks to see if there is a play at second base.

Bunt Defense with a Runner
at Third Base Drill

Objective:

To improve the infielders' ability to execute the bunt defense with a runner at third base.

Set-Up for All Rounds:

The pitcher, catcher, first baseman, second baseman, third baseman, and shortstop are at their defensive positions.

Half of the players are at home plate as hitters, while the other half of the players serve as baserunners.

The head coach is in the third base coaching box, and the assistant coach is in the first base coaching box.

Directions:

Round 1:

The defense fields the bunt, checks the runner at third base, and throws the ball to first base. The second baseman, who has taken the throw at first base, throws the ball home to get out the runner, who has broken for home.

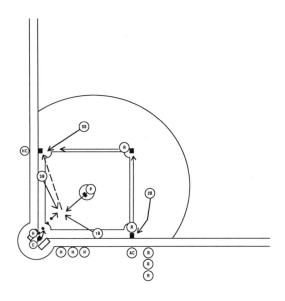

Round 3

Bunt Defense with Runners
at First and Second Bases Drill

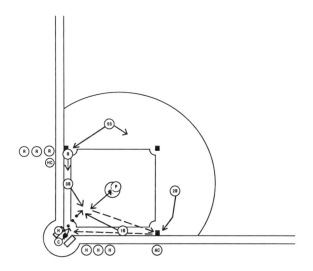

Round 1

Bunt Defense with a Runner
at Third Base Drill

Bunt Defense with a Runner
at Third Base Drill
(Continued)

Round 2:

The defense fields the bunt, fakes a throw to first base, and throws the ball to third base to get out the runner, who has initiated a move for home.

Round 3:

The defense fields the bunt and throws the ball to home plate to get out the runner, who has tried to advance home on a squeeze play.

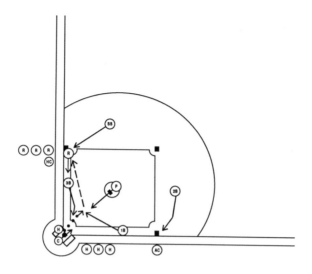

Round 2

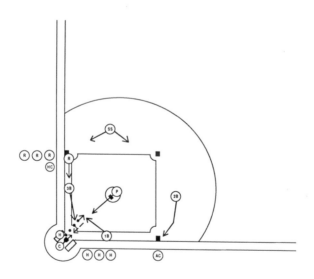

Round 3

Bunt Defense with a Runner
at Third Base Drill

From using the drills contained in this chapter, your infielders should improve on the following:

1. Executing the bunt defense with a runner at first base
2. Executing the bunt defense with a runner at second base
3. Executing the bunt defense with runners at first and second bases
4. Executing the bunt defense with a runner at third base
5. Executing the bunt defense for a squeeze play with a runner at first base
6. Executing the bunt defense for a squeeze play with a runner at third base

12

Advanced Technique Drills

Drills for improving the following advanced techniques are presented in this chapter:
1. Executing pick-off plays at first, second, and third bases
2. Executing the rundown play
3. Defending the double steal with different options

Pick-Off Play Drill

Objective:

To improve the catcher's ability to execute pick-off plays at first and third bases.

Set-Up:

Pitcher, catcher, first baseman, second baseman, third baseman, and shortstop are at their defensive positions.

Drill has three to four runners at first and third bases.

Directions:

The pitcher pitches a ball to the catcher. On the release of the pitch, the runner at first base takes an aggressive lead, while the second baseman breaks hard to first base. The catcher then throws the pick-off to first base.

The pitcher pitches a ball to the catcher. On the release of the pitch, the runner at third base takes an aggressive lead, while the shortstop breaks hard to third base. The catcher then throws the pick-off to third base.

NOTE: FULL PROTECTIVE CATCHING GEAR SHOULD BE WORN BY THE CATCHER FOR THIS DRILL.

Coaching Hint:

On a specific pick-off, to either first base or third base, the first baseman or third baseman should break toward home plate on the release of the pitch. This distracts the runner's attention and helps the second baseman or shortstop to come in from behind.

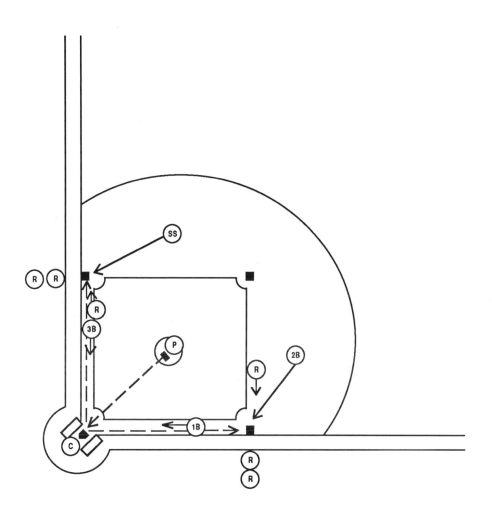

Pick-Off Play Drill

Catcher to First Base Pick-Off Drill

Objective:

To improve the catcher's execution of the pick-off play at first base.

Set-Up:

Pitcher, catcher, first baseman, second baseman, third baseman, and shortstop are at their defensive positions.

Drill has two or more runners at first base.

Directions:

The first baseman moves back toward first base for the pick-off play before the pitch is released. The pitcher pitches the ball to the catcher. On the release of the pitch, the runner at first base takes an aggressive lead, while the first baseman breaks hard to first base. The catcher then throws the pick-off to first base.

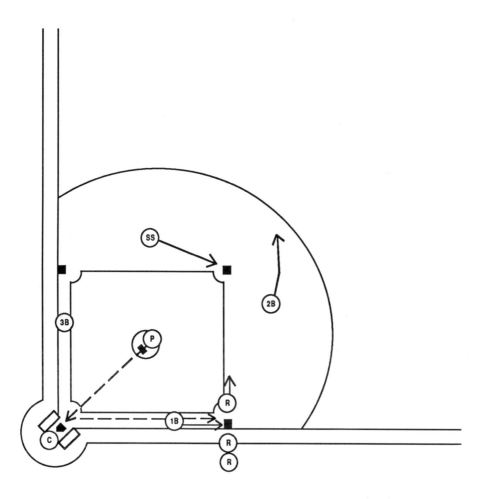

Catcher to First Base Pick-Off Drill

Pitcher to Second Base Pick-Off Drill

Objective:

To improve the pitcher's execution of the pick-off play at second base.

Set-Up:

Pitcher, catcher, first baseman, second baseman, third baseman, and shortstop are at their defensive positions.

Drill has two or more runners at second base.

Directions:

The pitcher pitches the ball to the catcher. On the release of the pitch, the runner at second base takes an aggressive lead, while the second baseman breaks hard to second base. The catcher throws the ball back to the pitcher. The pitcher pivots and throws the ball to second base for the out.

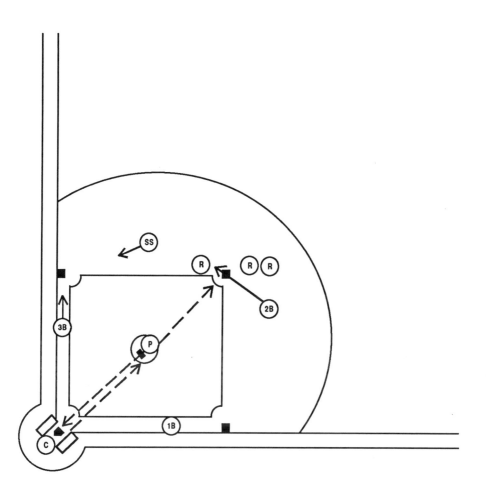

Pitcher to Second Base Pick-Off Drill

Pitcher to Third Base Pick-Off Drill

Objective:

To improve the pitcher's execution of the pick-off play at third base.

Set-Up:

Pitcher, catcher, first baseman, second baseman, third baseman, and shortstop are at their defensive positions.

Drill has two or more runners at third base.

Directions:

The pitcher pitches a ball to the catcher. On the release of the pitch, the runner at third base takes an aggressive lead, while the shortstop breaks hard to third base. The catcher throws the ball back to the pitcher. The pitcher pivots and throws the ball to third base for the out.

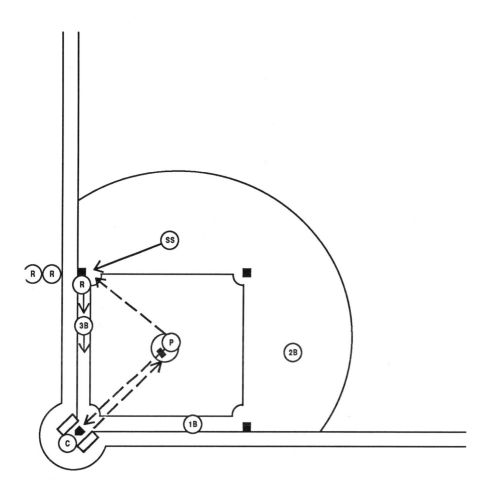

Pitcher to Third Base Pick-Off Drill

One-Throw Rundown Drill

Objective:

To practice executing the rundown play.

Set-Up:

The first baseman and two third basemen are at their respective bases. The second baseman and shortstop are at second base, while the catcher is at the defensive position.

Drill has three or more runners at each base.

Drill has three tossers. Tosser 1 is near the pitching area and halfway between first base and second base. Tosser 2 is near the pitching area and halfway between second base and third base. Tosser 3 is near the pitching area and halfway between third base and home plate.

Directions:

The runner at first base runs halfway between first base and second base. Tosser 1 throws the ball to the shortstop, who is moving in the direction of the runner. The shortstop chases the runner back to first base and either tags the runner or tosses the ball to the first baseman for the tag play.

The same drill sequence occurs at second base and third base with the second baseman taking the throw at second base and the third baseman taking the throw at third base.

Coaching Hint:

If the drill is performed correctly, it causes the runner to be "safe or out" at the base from which the runner started.

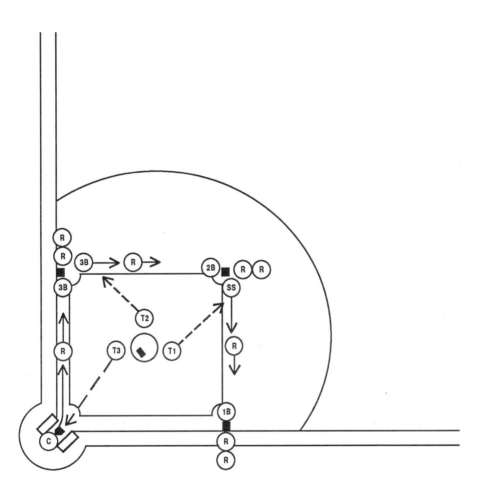

One-Throw Rundown Drill

Pick-Off with Rundown Drill

Objective:

To improve the execution of the pick-off and rundown plays.

Set-Up:

Pitcher, catcher, first baseman, second baseman, third baseman, and shortstop are at their defensive positions.

Drill has three or more runners at first base.

Directions:

The pitcher pitches a ball to the catcher. On the release of the pitch, the runner at first base takes an aggressive lead, while the second baseman breaks hard to first base. The catcher throws the pick-off to first base.

The runner is now caught in a rundown situation. The second baseman runs toward the runner causing the runner to commit running toward second base. As the runner reaches the halfway point between the bases, the second baseman throws the ball to the short-stop, who is moving in the direction of the runner. The shortstop chases the runner back to first base and either tags the runner or tosses the ball to the first baseman for the tag play.

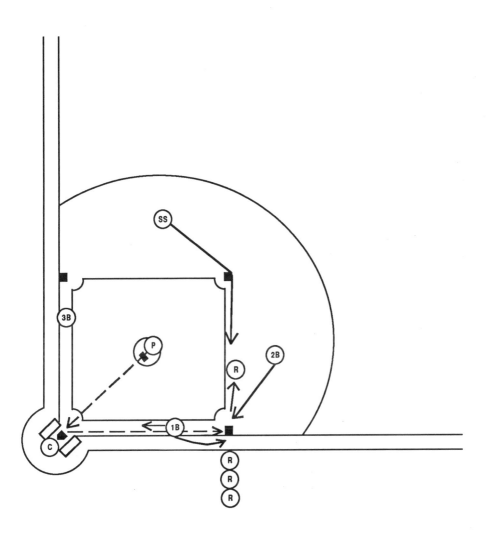

Pick-Off with Rundown Drill

Defending the Double Steal Drill

Objective:

To improve the player's execution of different options used in defending the double steal.

Set-Up for Double Steal Options 1-6:

Pitcher, catcher, first baseman, second baseman, third baseman, and shortstop are at their defensive positions.

Drill has two or more runners at first and third bases.

Directions:

Option 1:

The pitcher pitches a ball to the catcher. The catcher checks the runner at third base and throws the ball in a line to second base. The second baseman breaks to the mid-point between second base and the pitcher. At the same time, the third baseman breaks back to third base. The second baseman intercepts the ball and throws to either the third baseman, who catches the runner off base, or throws to home plate to get the runner, who has broken for home.

Option 2:

The pitcher pitches a ball to the catcher. The catcher checks the runner at third base and throws the ball in a line to second base. The shortstop breaks to the mid-point between second base and the pitcher. At the same time, the third baseman breaks back to third base. The shortstop intercepts the ball and throws to either the third baseman, who catches the runner off base, or throws to home plate to get the runner, who has broken for home.

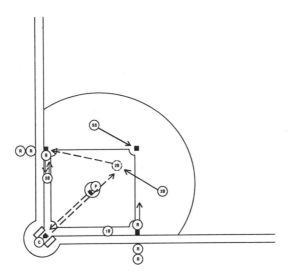

Option 1

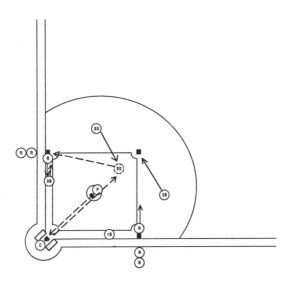

Option 2

Defending the Double Steal Drill

Defending the Double Steal Drill
(Continued)

Option 3:
The pitcher pitches a ball to the catcher. The catcher checks the runner at third base and throws the ball in a line to second base. The second baseman breaks to the mid-point between second base and the pitcher. At the same time, the third baseman breaks back to third base. The second baseman intercepts the ball, checks third base, and realizing the runner has not taken a big lead, flips the ball back to the shortstop, who is covering second base. The shortstop is now in a rundown situation with the runner at first base. At any point that the shortstop realizes the runner at third base has broken for home, the shortstop throws to home for the out. If the runner at third base does not break for home, the shortstop tries to get the runner out at first base.

Option 4:
The pitcher pitches a ball to the catcher. The catcher checks the runner at third base and throws the ball to second base for the out. The shortstop takes the throw at second base, while the second baseman moves to the mid-point between second base and the pitcher. The second baseman moves to this position to intercept bad throws to second base.

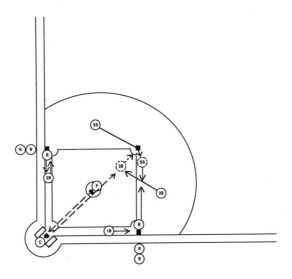

Option 3

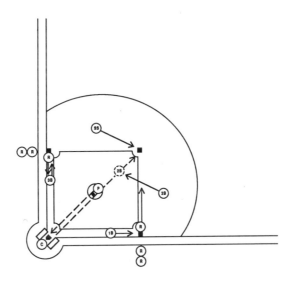

Option 4

Defending the Double Steal Drill

Defending the Double Steal Drill
(Continued)

Option 5:

The pitcher pitches a ball to the catcher. On the release of the pitch, the third baseman breaks back to third base. The catcher throws the ball directly to the third baseman for the out. The shortstop backs up the throw at third base, and the second baseman covers second base.

Option 6:

The pitcher pitches a ball to the catcher. At the same time, the third baseman breaks back to third base. The catcher throws the ball directly to the pitcher. The pitcher pivots and throws to the third baseman for the out. The shortstop covers second base, while the second baseman serves as the backup.

Variation:

The pitcher throws the ball to second base for the out.

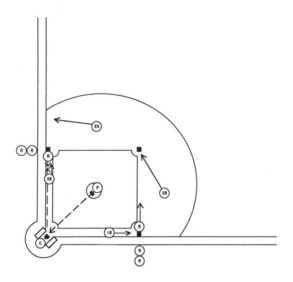

Option 5

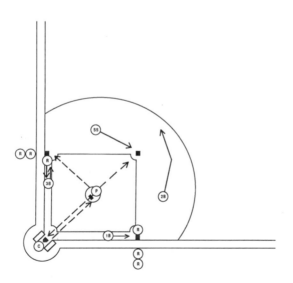

Option 6

Defending the Double Steal Drill

From using the drills contained in this chapter, your athletes should improve on the following:

1. Executing pick-off plays at first, second, and third bases
2. Executing the rundown play
3. Defending the double steal with different options

13

Pre-Game Warm-Up Drills

Objective for Pre-Game Warm-Up Drills:

To allow the players to practice in a game-like situation prior to the regularly scheduled game.

Set-Up for Pre-Game Warm-Up Drills:

The players are at their defensive positions, except for the first baseman and third baseman, who are at their respective bases. The catcher does not assume the defensive position until the outfielders begin throwing the ball to home plate. The drills have one or more players at each position.

The head coach serves as the hitter and is in the infield behind the pitching area for all outfield series drills. The shagger stands on either side of the head coach depending on the outfielder the coach is hitting to.

The pre-game warm-up drills are divided into two sections.
Section 1 contains the following outfield series:
1. Outfield throwing to the cut-off
2. Outfield throwing to the bases
3. Outfield throwing to home plate

Section 2 contains the following infield series:
1. Infield throwing combination
2. Infield throwing to first base with a throw back from the catcher
3. Infield double play
4. Infield throwing to third base
5. Infield throwing to home plate and coming in

Section 1: Outfield Series

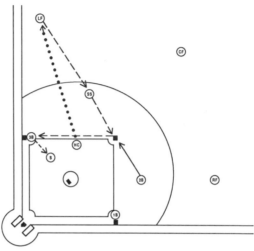

The head coach hits two ground balls to the left fielder with the shortstop lined up in the cut-off position with second base. On the first ground ball, the left fielder throws the ball in a line to second base with the shortstop cutting the ball off and relaying it to second base. On the second ground ball, the left fielder throws the ball directly to second base. The second baseman throws the ball to third base, and the third baseman throws the ball to the shagger.

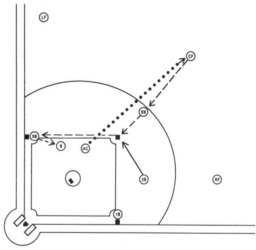

The head coach hits two ground balls to the center fielder with the shortstop lined up in the cut-off position with second base. On the first ground ball, the center fielder throws the ball in a line to second base with the shortstop cutting the ball off and relaying it to second base. On the second ground ball, the center fielder throws the ball directly to second base. The second baseman throws the ball to third base, and the third baseman throws the ball to the shagger.

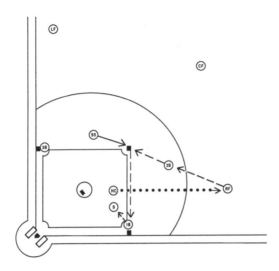

The head coach hits two ground balls to the right fielder with the second baseman lined up in the cut-off position with second base. On the first ground ball, the right fielder throws the ball in a line to second base with the second baseman cutting the ball off and relaying it to second base. On the second ground ball, the right fielder throws the ball directly to second base. The shortstop throws the ball to first base, and the first baseman throws the ball to the shagger.

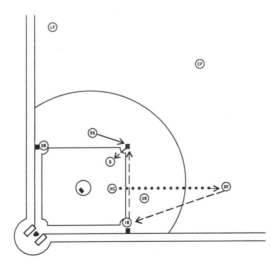

The head coach hits two ground balls to the right fielder, who throws both balls to first base. The first baseman throws the balls to second base with the shortstop taking the throws. The shortstop throws the balls to the shagger.

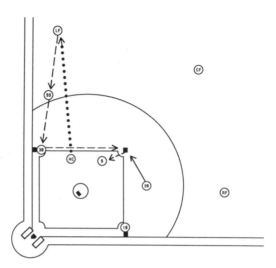

The head coach hits two ground balls to the left fielder with the shortstop lined up in the cut-off position with third base. On the first ground ball, the left fielder throws the ball in a line to third base with the shortstop cutting the ball off and relaying it to third base. On the second ground ball, the left fielder throws the ball directly to third base. The third baseman throws the ball to second base, and the second baseman throws it to the shagger.

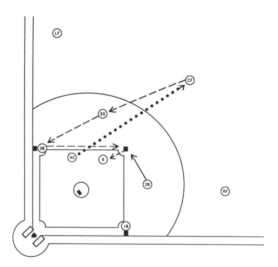

The head coach hits two ground balls to the center fielder with the shortstop lined up in the cut-off position with third base. On the first ground ball, the center fielder throws the ball in a line to third base with the shortstop cutting the ball off and relaying it to third base. On the second ground ball, the center fielder throws the ball directly to third base. The third baseman throws the ball to second base, and the second baseman throws the ball to the shagger.

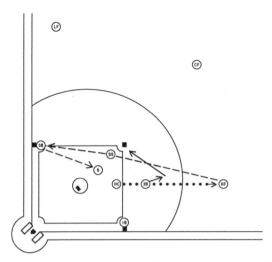

The head coach hits two ground balls to the right fielder with the shortstop lined up in the cut-off position with third base. On the first ground ball, the right fielder throws the ball in a line to third base with the shortstop cutting the ball off and relaying it to third base. On the second ground ball, the right fielder throws the ball directly to third base. The third baseman throws the ball to the shagger.

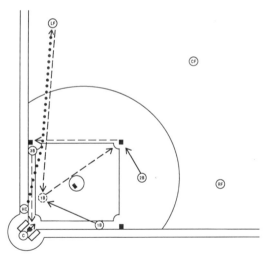

The head coach, who is in the vicinity of home plate, hits two ground balls to the left fielder with the first baseman lined up in a cut-off position with home plate. On the first ground ball, the left fielder throws the ball in a line to home plate. On the command of the catcher, the first baseman cuts the ball off and relays it to second base. The second baseman throws the ball to third base and the third baseman throws the ball to the catcher. On the second ground ball, the left fielder throws the ball directly to home plate.

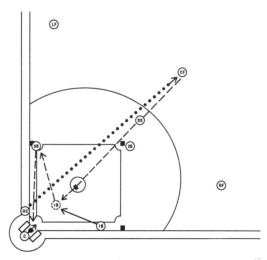

The head coach, who is in the vicinity of home plate, hits two ground balls to the center fielder with the first baseman lined up in a cut-off position with home plate. On the first ground ball, the center fielder throws the ball in a line to home plate. On the command of the catcher, the first baseman cuts the ball off and relays it to third base. The third baseman throws the ball to the catcher. On the second ground ball, the center fielder throws the ball directly to home plate.

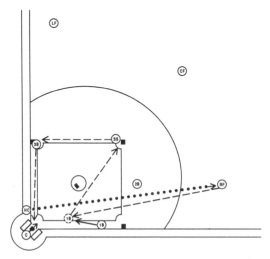

The head coach, who is in the vicinity of home plate, hits two ground balls to the right fielder with the first baseman lined up in a cut-off position with home plate. On the first ground ball, the right fielder throws the ball in a line to home plate. On the command of the catcher, the first baseman cuts the ball off and relays it to second base. The shortstop throws the ball to third base, and the third baseman throws the ball to the catcher. On the second ground ball, the right fielder throws the ball directly to home plate.

Section 2: Infield Series

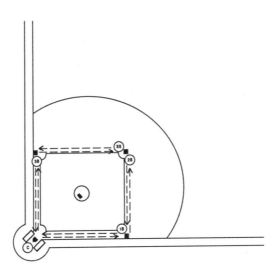

See the directions for Around the Horn and Reverse Throwing Drill, page 42.

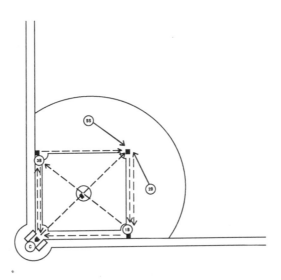

See directions for Double Play Drill #2, page 56.

NOTE: THE HEAD COACH SERVES AS THE HITTER AND IS AT HOME PLATE FOR THE REMAINING INFIELD SERIES DRILLS.

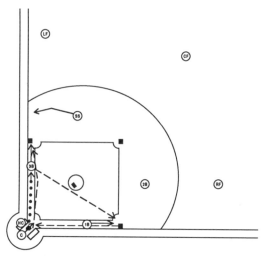

The head coach hits a ground ball to the third baseman, who fields the ball and throws it to first base. The first baseman throws the ball to the catcher. The catcher throws the ball to third base with the third baseman covering the base. The third baseman throws the ball back to the catcher.

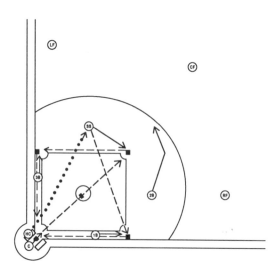

The head coach hits a ground ball to the shortstop, who fields the ball and throws it to first base. The first baseman throws the ball to the catcher. The catcher throws the ball to second base with the short-stop covering the base. The shortstop throws the ball back to third base, and the third baseman throws the ball to the catcher.

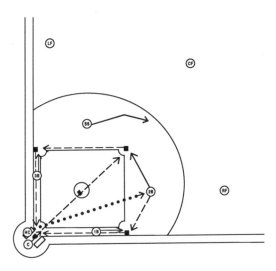

The head coach hits a ground ball to the second baseman, who fields the ball and throws it to first base. The first baseman throws the ball to the catcher. The catcher throws the ball to second base with the second baseman covering the base. The second baseman throws the ball to third base, and the third baseman throws the ball back to the catcher.

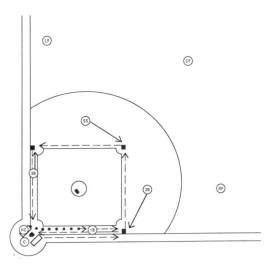

The head coach hits a ground ball to the first baseman, who fields the ball and throws it to first base with the second baseman covering the base. The second baseman throws the ball to the catcher. The catcher throws the ball back to first base with the first baseman covering the base. The first baseman throws the ball to second base with the shortstop covering the base. The shortstop throws the ball to third base, and the third baseman throws the ball to the catcher.

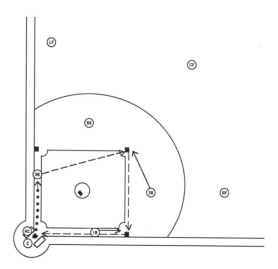

The head coach hits a ground ball to the third baseman. The third baseman throws the ball to second base with the second baseman turning the double play to first base. The first baseman throws the ball to the catcher.

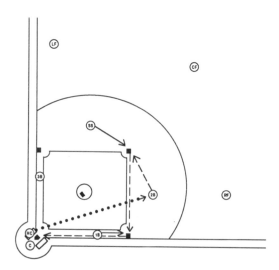

The head coach hits a ground ball to the second baseman. The second baseman throws the ball to second base with the shortstop turning the double play to first base. The first baseman throws the ball to the catcher.

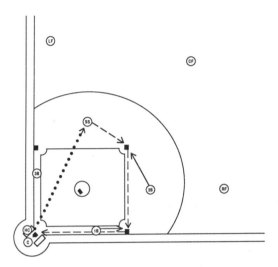

The head coach hits a ground ball to the shortstop. The shortstop throws the ball to second base with the second baseman turning the double play to first base. The first baseman throws the ball to the catcher.

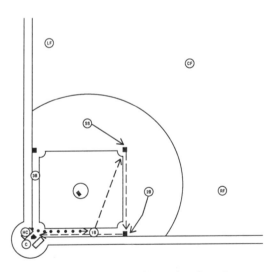

The head coach hits a ground ball to the first baseman. The first baseman throws the ball to second base with the shortstop turning the double play to first base. The second baseman throws the ball to the catcher.

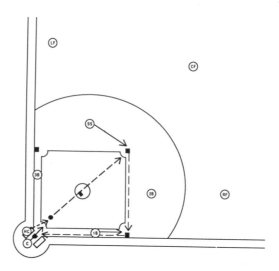

The head coach rolls a ball in front of home plate. The catcher fields the ball and throws the ball to second base with the shortstop turning the double play to first base. The first baseman throws the ball to the catcher.

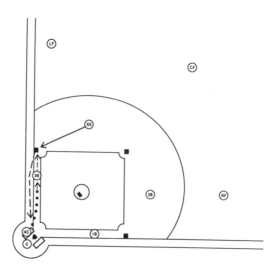

The head coach hits a ground ball to the third baseman. The third baseman throws the ball to third base with the shortstop covering the base. The shortstop throws the ball to the catcher.

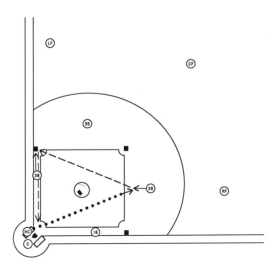

The head coach hits a ground ball to the second baseman. The second baseman throws the ball to third base. The third baseman throws the ball to the catcher.

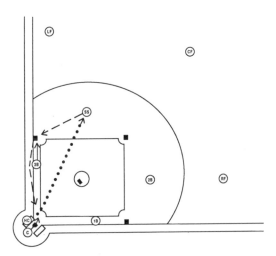

The head coach hits a ground ball to the shortstop. The shortstop throws the ball to third base. The third baseman throws the ball to the catcher.

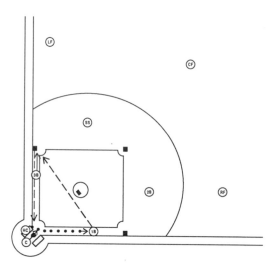

The head coach hits a ground ball to the first baseman. The first baseman throws the ball to third base. The third baseman throws the ball to the catcher.

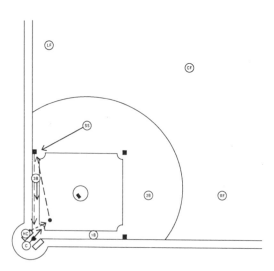

The head coach rolls a ball in front of home plate. The catcher fields the ball and throws the ball to third base with the shortstop covering the base. The shortstop throws the ball to the catcher.

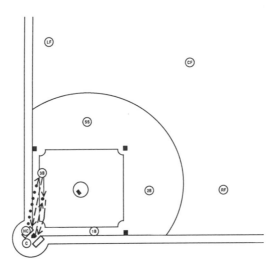

The head coach hits a ground ball to the third baseman. The third baseman throws the ball to the catcher. The catcher rolls a ball toward the third baseman, who charges the ball and throws it home.

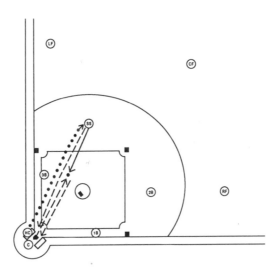

The head coach hits a ground ball to the shortstop. The shortstop throws the ball to the catcher. The catcher rolls a ball toward the shortstop, who charges the ball and throws it home.

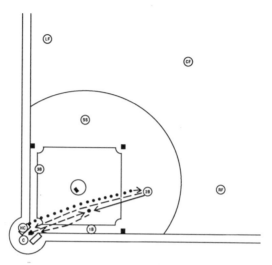

The head coach hits a ground ball to the second baseman. The second baseman throws the ball to the catcher. The catcher rolls a ball toward the second baseman, who charges the ball and throws it home.

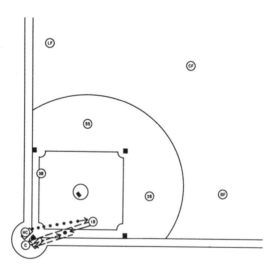

The head coach hits a ground ball to the first baseman. The first baseman throws the ball to the catcher. The catcher rolls a ball toward the first baseman, who charges the ball and throws it home.

FROM USING THE PRE-GAME WARM-UP DRILLS IN THIS CHAPTER, YOUR ATHLETES SHOULD ESTABLISH A SENSE OF READINESS PRIOR TO THE REGULARLY SCHEDULED GAME.

14

Off-Season Conditioning Programs

The past decade has seen some remarkable performances in athletics. Many factors have undoubtedly contributed to these performances, but it is the belief of many coaches that one of the main contributors has been improvement in training methods. Coaches are continuously searching for the optimal conditioning program that will increase strength and flexibility, improve cardiovascular fitness, and require only a reasonable amount of work-out time and equipment.

To be successful against today's competition, a ballplayer must be in excellent physical condition. In order for the athlete to stay in good physical condition throughout the year, the following programs can be used for off-season conditioning.

Interval Conditioning Program

The interval conditioning program is designed to increase the athlete's running speed. It is important that the athlete be given the full recovery period between repetitions and sets.

Repetitions	Distance	Speed	Recovery Between Reps.	Recovery Between Sets
1	880 meters	warm-up	— — —	— — —
1	100 meters	accelerate speed - 3 times	— — —	— — —
3	30 meters	one-half speed	2 minutes	4 minutes
3	30 meters	full speed	2 minutes	4 minutes
3	60 meters	full speed	2 minutes	4 minutes
3	30 meters	full speed	2 minutes	4 minutes
1	880 meters	cool down	— — —	— — —

Circuit Conditioning Program

The circuit conditioning program is composed of aerobic activities, plyometric exercises, and explosive power exercises. The circuit is a 30-45 minute non-stop conditioning program, which consists of 12 exercise stations. The stations can be performed in any order with the cool down station performed at the end of the program. Also, the stations can be varied depending on your facilities and the fitness level of your athletes. The circuit should be performed by partners with comparable strength and speed. In order to get maximum effort from the athletes, each individual can be timed on how long it takes to perform the circuit.

Circuit Conditioning Program

Station	Repetitions
1. Running Laps 880 meters	1
2. Square Drill a. Sprint length of gym. b. Run backwards for width of gym. c. Grapevine the length of gym. (Right over left foot; right behind left foot.) d. Walk the width of gym to start again.	5
3. Medicine Ball Jumps Start medicine ball (6-9 pound ball) at chest level; raise ball over head with every jump.	15
4. Bench Step-ups Right foot up; left foot up. Right foot down; left foot down.	50
5. Push-ups	20
6. Running Up Stairs First repetition, run one step at a time. Second repetition, run two steps at a time. Alternate for remaining repetitions. Walk down between each flight.	10
7. Depth Jumping Stand on bench (0.40m bench); step off, as soon as contact is made with the floor, jump up as high as possible off both feet; use arms to explode upward.	15
8. Rope Jumping Jump off both feet.	120
9. Reaction Running	2

5 FT.   10 FT.   15 FT.   20 FT.   30 FT.

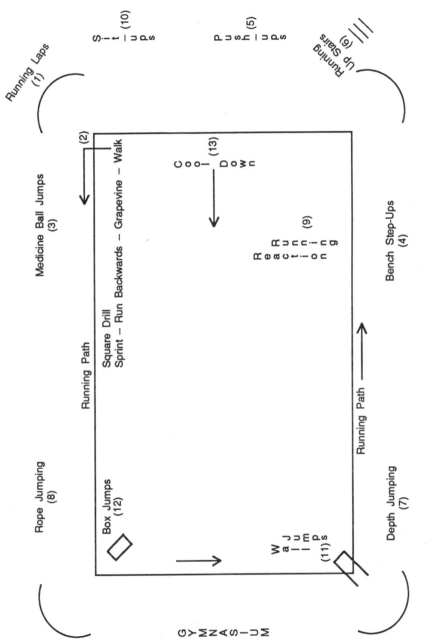

Running Laps (1)

Sit-Ups (10)

Push-Ups (5)

Running Up Stairs (6)

Medicine Ball Jumps (3)

Running Path

Square Drill
Sprint – Run Backwards – Grapevine – Walk (2)

Cool Down (13)

Reaction Running (9)

Bench Step-Ups (4)

Rope Jumping (8)

Box Jumps (12)

Wall Jumps (11)

Running Path

Depth Jumping (7)

GYMNASIUM

Circuit Conditioning Program

10. Sit-ups   30
    V sit-ups (both arms and legs come
    together to form a "V").

11. Wall Jumps   60
    Stand at door opening; jump and touch
    top of door frame continuously with
    both hands.

12. Box Jumps or Rope Jumps   2 x 30
    Jump continuously over box
    or jump rope.

13. Cool Down
    Jog slowly up and down the gym.

Individualized Conditioning Program

The individualized conditioning program is designed to improve the athlete's physical condition on an individual basis. The program provides the athlete with a wide variety of activities to meet the desired training goals. Also, the individualized conditioning program places some of the responsibility for conditioning on the athlete. It is the athlete's responsibility to determine the conditioning goals and to select appropriate activities to meet those goals.

*Goal Per Month: minimum of 45 points

Events	Points Earned
1. Aerobics	1. 1 per day/1 hour program
2. Weights	2. 1 per week/3 day program
3. Circuit Conditioning	3. 1 per day/30-45 min. program
4. Running	4. 3 per week/3 day program
5. Swimming	5. 3 per week/3 day program
6. Cycling	6. 1 per 25 miles
7. Batting	7. 1 per 80 hits & 45 bunts
8. Pitching	8. 1 per 150 pitches
9. Grounders	9. 1 per 125 grounders
10. Throwing	10. 1 per 150 throws

*The coach must evaluate the physical conditioning levels of the athletes and develop running and swimming programs to fit their needs.

The following is a tally sheet that can be used by the athlete for recording the points earned each week.

Tally Sheet

Name _____

	Monday	Tuesday	Wednesday	Thursday	Friday	Saturday	Sunday
1. Aerobics							
2. Weights							
3. Circuit							
4. Running							
5. Swimming							
6. Cycling							
7. Batting							
8. Pitching							
9. Grounders							
10. Throwing							

The following are some suggested guidelines for using the individualized conditioning program:

1. The athlete should earn two points per week performing aerobics and one point per week lifting weights.
2. The athlete should select running, swimming, or cycling, or do a combination of the three events. If the athlete does one-half the workout of one event, the athlete gets one-half the points.
3. Running, swimming, and cycling can be done on the athlete's own time. However, if the athlete is not a self-motivated person, then the workout should be performed with a partner.
4. The batting program consists of 80 hits and 45 bunts. The athlete may use the batting tees, sock balls, batting machine, etc. to achieve this goal.
5. The minimum time for each athlete's workout should be 2½ hours per day.
6. The athlete should record earned points on the tally sheet. Credit should not be recorded until the activity has been completed.
7. On Monday morning, the athlete should turn in the points earned for the previous week, so the coach can keep a weekly record of the team's progress.
8. The athlete should turn in the tally sheet at the end of each month.
9. At the end of each month, the athlete should have earned 45 points. If fewer than 45 points are achieved, the deficient points are carried over to the next month's points. You might want to establish an award system for the athlete who achieves over 45 points per month.

NOTE: You may need to adjust the above guidelines to meet the needs of your athletes.

FROM USING THE CONDITIONING PROGRAMS PRESENTED IN THIS CHAPTER, YOUR ATHLETES SHOULD MAINTAIN A GOOD LEVEL OF PHYSICAL CONDITION THROUGHOUT THE YEAR.